Walks around Charnwood

A FOOTPATH GUIDE

Heather MacDermid

CORDEE BOOKS - LEICESTER

CORDEE BOOKS
3a De Montfort Street, Leicester LE1 7HD

Published by Cordee 1986

Copyright © Heather MacDermid 1985
Maps Cordee

All rights reserved. No part of this publications may be reproduced, stored in a retrieval system, or transmitted, in any form or by any means, without prior permission of the publisher.

British Library Cataloguing in Publication Data

MacDermid, Heather
  Walks around Charnwood.
  1. Charnwood Forest (England) — Description and travel — Guide-books
  1. Title
  914.25'4704858   DA670.C44
  ISBN 0-904405-13-3

Produced in Great Britain by the Ernest Press

Acknowledgements

I should like to acknowledge my debt of gratitude:

to Mr A. Squires whose kind help and meticulous attention to detail has saved me from many errors and misinterpretations in the historical section of this book

to Mr. G. Farmham and to Mr. M. Curzon-Herrick for permission to use material under their copyright in Leicester Records Office

to Leicester museum staff for their unfailing courtesy in answering queries

to the Record Office for providing assistance in access to historical material

to Pete Byfield, woodman extraordinary, for his tutorials on the history of woodland management

to my friends in LFA who have kindly 'fool-proofed' the instructions for walking

to my daughter, Catriona, for reading the text with a critical eye and evident interest

and to M.D. Essinger for assistance in proof-reading.

Illustrations by Jean Harrison.

Maps and cover design by Ivan Cumberpatch.

CONTENTS

Walks: Key Map 4
       Introduction 5
Preface 7
The Story of Charnwood and its Footpaths 9
Bradgate Park 22
       Introductory Walk 26
Walk 1 Branching out from Bradgate 28
       The Quorn Extension 35
Walk 2 The Heart of the Forest 39
Walk 3 From Copt Oak out to the Outwoods 47
Walk 4 From Copt Oak West Towards Whitwick 56
Walk 5 From Whitwick in Search of an Extinct Volcano ... 63

WAYS IN TO CHARNWOOD

Way In From **Leicester** 73
Way In From **Groby** 79
Way In From **Markfield** 83
Way In From **Whitwick** 89
Way In From **Loughborough** 91
Samuel Wyld's "Perambulations Round Charnwood
               Forrest 1754" 95
Bibliography 96

Key Map

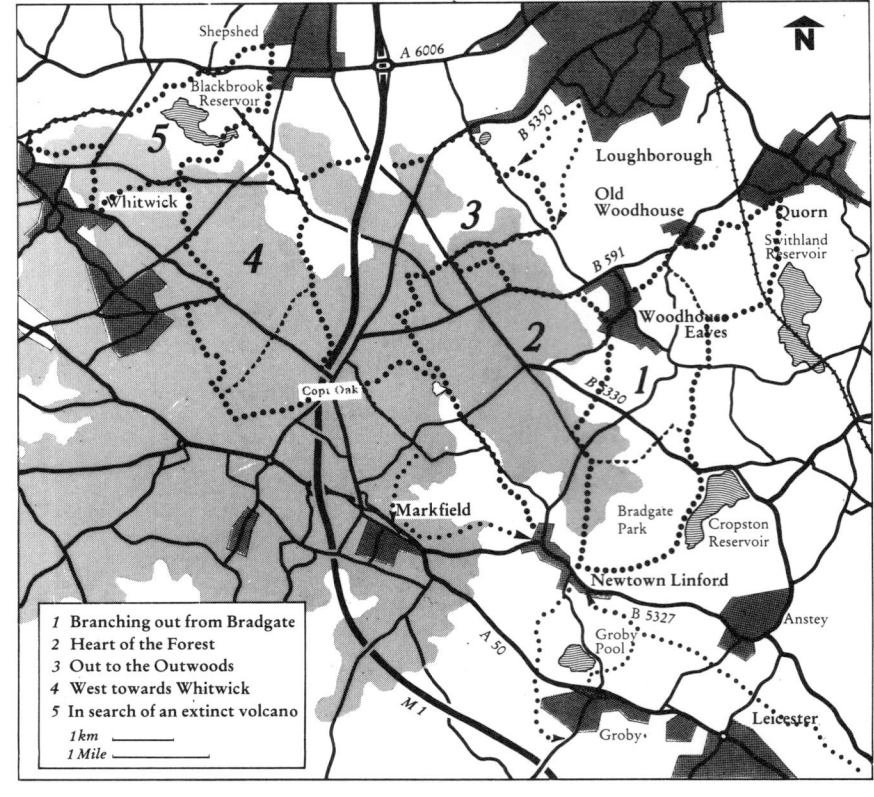

1. Branching out from Bradgate
2. Heart of the Forest
3. Out to the Outwoods
4. West towards Whitwick
5. In search of an extinct volcano

The Walks

The walks begin with a tour of Bradgate, for those who are not already familiar with the beauty spots of the park. In holiday periods the main car parks can be crowded. Tourists can block the main street of Newtown Linford. The main drive through the park can seem like the promenade of a busy seaside holiday resort. But, once away from the park gates and the metalled drive, you can find peace and calm in the bracken-covered hills. In winter, especially mid-week, even the main routes can be quiet. And at all times, it is beautiful.

INTRODUCTORY STROLL AROUND BRADGATE....

A gentle 4 mile walk, familiarizing yourself with the landmarks of Bradgate Park. This can be done with babies, toddlers, grandparents and even reluctant teenagers.

Walk 1. BRANCHING OUT FROM BRADGATE..

To Woodhouse Eaves and Swithland Woods. 6 miles if you start from Hunt's Hill car park: 9 miles from Newton Linford. There is an optional extra 3 miles to Quorn.

It is possible to purchase food and drink on this walk, at Woodhouse Eaves (but don't rely on refreshments at Swithland. The only eating place is the Griffin pub, which is a mile along the road from the footpath route.) There are lots of tempting places to loiter in or explore, so allow plenty of time and have a good day out!

Walk 2. THE HEART OF THE FOREST ....

From Newtown Linford to Ulverscroft Priory, Charley Chapel, Bawdon Castle, Beacon Hill, Broombriggs, Maplewell, Hunt's Hill and Newtown. The priory is a ruin, the chapel no longer a chapel and the castle was never a castle but the walk is delightful and the views magnificent. A good 10 miles, with no commercial tea breaks once you leave Newtown Linford: so take a picnic, unless you prefer to walk into Woodhouse Eaves from Maplewell. It's not a long detour and the amentities there are very civilised.

Walk 3. FROM COPT OAK OUT TO THE OUTWOODS

To Charley Hall, Cat Hill wood, Oaks in Charnwood, Lubcloud, Longcliffe, Nanpantan, The Outwoods, Pocket Gate, Deans lane, Beacon Hill, Ulverscroft Lodge,

A 10 mile circuit in an area of the Forest cruelly cut through by the M1 motorway. This has not destroyed the beauty of the landscape but it makes a noisy accompaniment to the walk at one point, until you climb the hill into the valley beyond it. Once over the motorway you regain secret, silent countryside.

The only places for public refreshment are at the Priory pub at Nanpantan unless you wish to make a 2 mile extension to refresh yourself at Woodhouse Eaves.

Walk 4. FROM COPT OAK WEST TOWARDS WHITWICK

To Rise Rocks, Bardon Hill, Agar Nook, Warren Hills, Mt. St. Bernard's Abbey, Oaks in Charnwood, Birch Hill wood.

An 8½ mile circuit with an optional 1 mile extension over a disputed path to Blackbrook Reservoir. This walk goes through the 'oldest' part of the Forest. The pre-Cambrian rocks, the result of ancient volcanic action are now quarry fodder and present some spectacular effects on the landscape so close to the peaceful and lonely Mt. St. Bernard's Abbey.

The Walks

It is possible to shorten this walk by starting from Agar Nook, Whitwick or Oaks in Charwood, omitting Copt Oak and using a shorter route from Burrow Wood to Old Rise Rocks, as described in a P.S. to the walk ....

Walk 5. FROM WHITWICK IN SEARCH OF AN EXTINCT VOLCANO

Possibly the most lovely part of the Forest. Whitwick itself, once an important castle and manor site, is now fallen from its former glory, but the countryside into which Whitwick folk can stroll is magnificent.

This route goes to Mt. St. Bernard's Abbey, close to the extinct volcano, now being quarried, and then across Blackbrook reservoir, along the disused Charnwood Forest railway, past the old Swanimote Rock and through Cademan Wood. The views of High Sharpley and Gun Hill are spectacular from various angles as you circle them.

There is the option of shortening the walk by omitting Thringstone and Cademan Wood.

Full route: 8 miles. Shortened route: 6½ miles.

The Ways In

1. From Leicester and back (4 miles each way)
2. From Groby and back (2 miles each way)
3. From Markfield and back (2 miles each way)
4. From Whitwick and back (2 miles — 1 mile)
5. From Loughborough and back (1 mile each way)

The Charnwood Circuit

This is the route for the long distance walker, who is looking for a challenging 33 mile circuit. It can be started from any of the walks, or added to any of the ways in.

			Page No.
Newtown Linford	Walk 2		
Ulverscroft Priory	Walk 2	2½ miles	42
Poultney Wood	Walk 3 (end)	½ mile	46
Copt Oak	Walk 4	1 mile	58
Rise Rocks	Walk 4	1¼ miles	58
Bardon Hill	Walk 4	1 mile	59
Agar Nook	Walk 4	1 mile	59
Mt. St Bernard's	Walk 4	2 miles	61
White Horse wood	Walk 5	2 miles	68
Poachers Corner	Walk 5	2 miles	69
Thringstone	Walk 5	1 mile	70
Cademan Wood	Walk 5	1 mile	70
Whitwick	Walk 5	1 mile	71
Mt. St. Bernard's	Walk 5	1 mile	67
Oaks in Charwood	Walk 3	1 mile by road 2 miles by field	51
Lubcloud	Walk 3	½ mile	51
Longcliffe	Walk 3	1 mile	52
Nanpantan	Walk 3	1 mile	52
The Outwoods	Walk 3	1 mile	52
Deans Lane	Walk 3	1 mile	52
Beacon Hill	Walk 2	1 mile	52
Woodhouse Eaves	Walk 1	1 mile	34
Woodhouse	Walk 1	1 mile	34
Quorn	Walk 1	1 mile	35
Rushall Field Farm	Walk 1	2 miles	37
Swithland	Walk 1	½ mile	38
Swithland Wood	Walk 1	1 mile	38
Bradgate Park	Introd. walk	2 miles	

Preface

This book has been written as an encouragement to walkers in exploring the ancient tracks and byways of Charnwood Forest. It began as a description of a 30-mile route around the edge of the Forest and it has mushroomed into a series of inner circuits within that route. The desire to provide 'ways in' from the neighbouring villages and towns led to the inclusion of short, circular walks to link up with the other routes. The result is a network of Charnwood Forest foot-paths, which will provide the keen walker with many a good day's rambling, away from main roads.

The paths described are little-used but well-established. Many of them are ancient rights of way between places of historical importance. They have all been recorded as definitive rights of way on the Ordnance Survey maps. We have a right to walk on them and our path should not be restricted or impeded. We have a corresponding duty to preserve them and to respect the land on each side of them.

The introductory ***Story of Charnwood and its footpaths*** is intended to foster an appreciation of the ancient rights of way which these footpaths record, and to give a general historical framework for an understanding of some of the features encountered on the way.

The Introductions to each walk indicate items of interest, places to stop, to start, to park a car, to catch a bus, to link up with other walks, to extend or shorten your route. They are meant to be read either before or after your walk or when you sit down to rest! They are intended: for those who like to be tempted to put on their boots and try paths they might not otherwise have ventured on,

for those who like to re-experience the delights of a ramble by reading about where they have walked

and for those whose imagination is great enough to give them the sensation of having walked these paths by reading the book from the comfort of their own armchair, without necessarily putting boot to soil!

Real walkers, who are impatient to start, can omit the rest and turn to the Instructions for walking......page 26.

The walks are all circular, so that car-owners can return to their starting point: but it is possible to leave the walks and take buses back to Leicester, Coalville or Loughborough from various places marked in the text.

The walks are based on one Grand Circuit of Charnwood (33 miles). Within that circuit are 5 shorter walks of 8 or 10 miles.

Leading into these walks are 5 'Ways In' which, on their own, make very pleasant little circular walks of 3 to 8 miles. Added to other walks, they make very satisfying 10, 12, 14 or 16 mile rambles.

The instructions for walking have been deliberately kept free of descriptions and explanations because the aim is to keep you on the right path with a minimum of distraction. Hopefully, you will be able to raise your eyes from the print at intervals to admire the views, without losing your place!

In adjoining circuits where the same ground is covered, instructions are given for both directions, as a walk always looks and feels so different when approached from a different angle. I hope that you will find, as I did, an added pleasure in walking paths that are half familiar from a previous walk in the other direction.

Preface

The route maps at the beginning of each walk are designed to give you a picture of the 'shape' of the walk, so that you can see at a glance the possibilities of variations you might choose.

The strip maps are a simplified version of the route maps. They go UP the page, as if they were unfolding under your feet, and are intended to illustrate the words and clarify the instructions.

The Ordnance Survey map for this area is S.K. 41/51 Pathfinder series 1;25000.

Distances given for walks in the text are approximations, measured by rule of thumb. (A good rambler's thumb measures 1 mile on O.S. Pathfinder maps. For increased accuracy, I measure miles in knots (with a string knotted at mile intervals using the scale on the map.) For smaller distances, I refer to yards, although I know this is an archaic measure. A yard equals one good ramblers' stride. The reader can, of course, make more accurate computations, using a fine mapping ruler, but for most purposes the kind of measurement given here is perfectly adequate to give you an idea of how long you need to allow, how much energy you will need and at what point you need to look for stiles or other crossing places.

The time required for a walk depends on your pace, but a good rough guide is to allow an hour for every two miles. The shorter walks of 8-10 miles in this book are designed to take about 4 or 5 hours. During the summer, this makes a good afternoon's walk, where you have long hours of daylight. In the winter, it's advisable to set off before lunch and make a day of it.

Planning your route. An evening spent with the book and a bus time-table to plan your escape routes to buses might be time well spent, especially if you are not sure of your walking capacity.

Buses are reasonably frequent to Newtown Linford, where the first two walks start and most of the other recommended starting points are serviced by the Midland Fox. The one exception is Copt Oak, which is not on a regular bus route. It is not far to walk from Copt Oak to Markfield, where there are buses.

Car-Parks. There are three car parks on the edges of Bradgate Park, which make useful starting and finishing places, as they provide toilets and refreshment and space to leave a car for a whole day for a very moderate fee. Most of the other recommended starting places have small car-parks, apart from Copt Oak, where you need to ask the landlord to allow you to use his car-park or find a quiet part of the road where your car will not be a nuisance.

Accommodation. If you wish to walk the whole outer circuit, taking several days, you may find accommodation at Copt Oak Youth Hostel or at hostelries in the 'Way In' towns and villages. Leicester Information Bureau provides lists of farmhouses offering bed and breakfast.

The possibilities and combinations of walks in the Forest are endless. Any of these described here can be started from any village or parking place marked on the map.

The Story of Charnwood and its Footpaths

Anyone approaching Leicester from the top of London Road sees, on a clear day, a beautiful view of the city below and of Bradgate Park beyond. The range of Charnwood hills makes a striking backdrop to most areas in the north and east of the city and it sometimes seems that everyone who lives near Leicester has, from their back doorstep or their bedroom window, a view of Old John.

Leicester people have a special affection for this beauty spot and Charnwood is probably the most well-known and well-loved place in Leicestershire.

It is variously described as 'a miniature Wales' or a 'little Matlock' by people who love those mountain landscapes: for although nowhere in Charnwood exceeds 912' in height, the rocky hills do give the impression of a highland scene.

The rocks are the very ancient results of tremendous volcanic activity. The great rocky outcrops and the dry stone walls made from them have a gaunt, imposing permanence about them. They give us the impression that these are landmarks which will remain for ever unchanged: that they will not be uprooted as trees and hedgerows are.

The casual visitor might well think that Charnwood is an example of an unchanging landscape and that here at least we shall not need to replace our Ordnance Survey maps every few years or to find our guide books out of date, as we do elsewhere in the county.

But of course it IS changing — very dramatically in some places. The dreaded oilseed rape has invaded the ancient meadowlands on the edge of the forest, and walls and boundary trees have been removed in many places.

A more violent rape of the landscape occurs with every quarry blast. The volcanic rocks of Bardon Hill have been shattered and scooped out so that only a shell remains. To the M1 motorist it still looks like an impressive hill but the rambler who tries to follow the path marked on his 1904 map or the 1971 book of **Walks in Leicestershire** sees that it is in fact only HALF a hill, with a spectacular drop from the summit down to the vast quarry below. Spring Hill, near Whitwick, and Longcliff and Buddon Wood have huge quarries, and Stanton under Bardon has recently extended its area of mineral extraction. Footpath walkers make great sweeps on diverted paths round these areas and they naturally lament the loss of old, direct routes from one landmark to another.

It is hard to live with these changes and to feel that urbanisation is destroying our rural heritage. It saddens me to hear the rumble of engines and machinery and the blasts of dynamite as I walk the field paths. And yet I know that the old, exhausted quarries where time has healed the scars and nature has re-established itself (as in Switaland and Lady Hay Wood) are now delightful places. It is in these lovely old former quarries that one becomes philosophical about the changes wrought by man. One grieves for the damage — and respects the capacity of nature to survive the affronts. But the huge scale of 20th century quarrying makes terrible inroads on the beauty spots and Charnwood's great strength is also her greatest weakness; for her pre-Cambrian rocks, the oldest and hardest in Britain, are very desirable as road core. The motorway which cuts through Charnwood is made from the rocks which are her greatest asset.

The River Lin. Bradgate Park

The Story of Charnwood and its Footpaths

This is perhaps the unkindest cut of all, for it is this motorway which brings another kind of danger to the peace and quiet of the countryside:- the tourist!

The motor car which brings increased numbers of visitors to Charnwood puts an undue burden on the area. And farmers are naturally hostile to an invasion of townsfolk who might damage their crops and animals.

Ramblers themselves do not want their peaceful walks disturbed by hordes of other walkers. We do not want the land eroded by a million feet, as on the few popular long-distance walks. This book is intended to encourage people to walk the less well-known paths so that the whole network of paths is preserved and maintained. There are many paths in the forest to spread those footsteps out. We do not need to confine ourselves to Bradgate and Beacon Hill!

We do have to remember that Charnwood is a very small area (only about 9 miles by 7) which cannot support the presence of too many people if it is to retain the charm of its rocky isolation.

Originally, of course, it was not the charm of the landscape which drew people to the area but the protection afforded by the high ground, and the usefulness of the natural resources (for the minerals were a valuable commodity even in ancient times). We have evidence that in the Bronze Age there were isolated settlements on Beacon Hill and in Buddon Wood, and that the Romans lived and worked in the Forest. But it must always have been difficult to wrest a living from the harsh terrain and it is only at the edges of the Forest that we find substantial settlement.

It was at Groby and Mountsorrel that the Romans quarried granite for their Leicester buildings and at places like Markfield, Groby, Thringstone and Whitwick that the Germanic invaders settled.

There are place names which indicate that the Danes settled here, (as they did in the eastern parts of the country, along the Wreake valley, where we find so many of the characteristic endings in "_by" in villages like Brooks**by**, Rother**by**, Fris**by**, and Gaddes**by**, etc.) Rat**by** and Gro**by**, Thringstone (formerly Thrings**by**) remind us that these villages on the outskirts of the Forest were also part of the Danelaw.

Evidence of settlement in the heart of the Forest is very thin indeed, but we can guess that the Saxons, who lay down much of the pattern of medieval farming, exploited the Forest while living on the fringes of it. (It may, indeed, have been a Royal hunting forest in Saxon times although it was not so, later).

Certainly, the four manors of Whitwick, Groby, Shepshed and Barrow were established before the Norman Conquest. In the Domesday Book they are described as having been given to four of William's Norman lords.

The story of Charnwood is usually described in relation to the history of the families who owned these manors, but I shall confine myself to those issues which concern the landscape and the footpaths......where the story becomes one of conflict between the demands of the land-lords and those of commoners for the rights of access over the land.

We are accustomed to the idea that all common land is now private property notwithstanding any rights of access over it: but the fact that there are such extensive rights over the common land indicates that in pre-feudal times there were rights

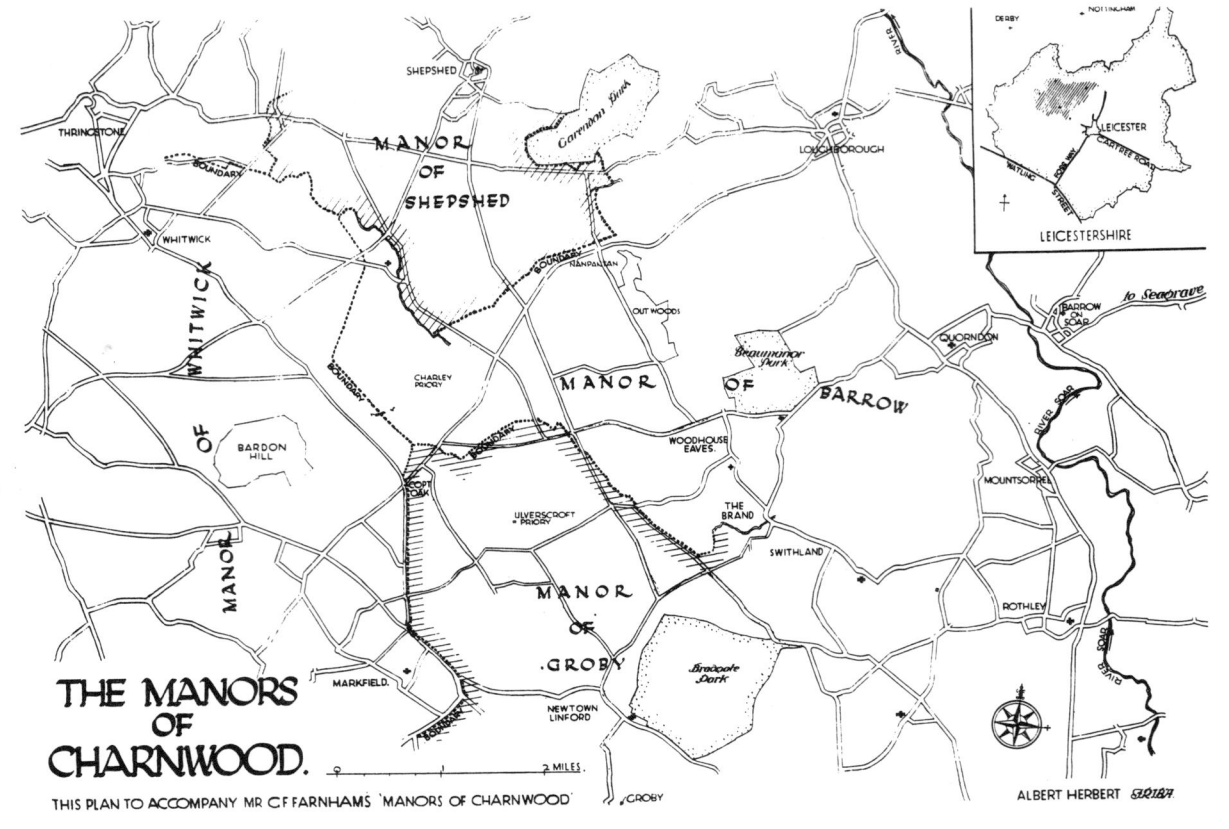

The Story of Charnwood and its Footpaths

that were much more extensive. W.G. Hoskins (***Common Lands of England and Wales***, 1963) claims that these rights are of 'vast antiquity' and probably ante-date the ideas of private property in land.

'The common rights (of grazing, fuel, cattle bedding) were not something granted by a generous landowner, but the residue of rights that were once much more extensive, probably older than the idea of private property in land'.

In Norman times, however the doctrine became established that all land belonged to the king, who rented it out or gave it as gifts in exchange for specified dues of loyalty, to favoured nobles. They in turn rented it out to tenants who paid them, usually with labour in working the land.

But as Hoskins suggests, the feudal owners were obliged to accept that there were ancient rights over the land that had previously always been held in common.

It was established that commoners (living in dwellings or on land which gave them rights on the Common land) were entitled to free pasturing of animals on the Common. They were also entitled to free access to their animals on the common land. Thus, the lord of the manor might claim to own the soil, the wood, the deer and his own animals; but the commoners, be they tenants or freemen, had equally important claims.

Indeed, the management of the land evolved as a delicate balance of interest between the lord and the commoners.

The picture that emerges of Charnwood in medieval times is of the four manors, on the edge of the Forest, at Whitwick, Groby, Shepshed and Barrow, each with its surrounding farmland. Beyond that lay the woods, which were a vital source of fuel and winter grazing: and beyond them, the area of unenclosed common, a mixture of shrub, heath, thicket, bog and woodland, which the Domesday Book calls 'the Waste' (a rather unfortunate term, considering the importance of it to the community!)

The 'wastes' of all four manors met in Charnwood.

In the 'waste' the lords of the manor could exercise their rights, of hunting, cutting down timber and other wood and of grazing their stock; and the commoners could graze stock and collect wood (but not kill deer or cut timber).

In the 12th century it became fashionable for the landlords to enclose parts of the 'waste' to make deer parks and to 'farm' the deer instead of leaving them to breed in the wild. The parks made it possible for the land to be used more profitably because although they were intended primarily for hunting, they also became important economically, in producing wool, fish, grazing, turf and minerals more efficiently than was possible on the 'waste'.

There was however much litigation about such enclosure of the common land, for commoners depended for their living on the grazing provided by the 'waste', and the law was established that the lord could only enclose land for his deer park provided that commoners were left enough land for their grazing.

The commoners' animals were branded and turned loose to graze on the 'waste' and rounded up at 'Drift' time, usually August/September and January (Holyrood Day and Twelfth Day) between harvest and planting. There were 'gates' or ways in to the Forest to allow the movement of stock between the

The Story of Charnwood and its Footpaths

village fields and the common land, and there were great Forest fences or park pales to keep the deer in the parks. **(One good example of a way of this kind is the K57 path to Pocket Gate from Loughborough, which was formerly hedged on both sides to allow free passage for stock through the parkland. There is also at Pocket Gate an embankment on the edge of the Outwoods which was once thought to be a part of the old deer-pale of Loughborough park land. There is a better example of old park pale visible on our path from Leicester to Anstey Pasture and one near Old Rise Rocks around Bardon, which was the medieval park for Whitwick manor).**

The wooded areas of the Common were essential to the economy throughout the medieval period, for the winter grazing of animals as well as for timber and wood for fuel and fencing. The problem is that these interests are incompatible and throughout medieval times the conflicting interests of hunting, grazing, farming and woodland management had to be carefully balanced for the agricultural system to work.

It was essential for everyone to feed their animals in woodland (acorns and beechmast provided quite important 'pannage' for pigs) and to collect animal bedding (of holly and elm) and deadwood ("by hook or by crook") for fuel; but it was equally important to have a continuous supply of trees growing for timber and fencing.

For regular and valuable timber for large scale building, trees need to be 80 to 100 years old and a certain proportion of trees need to be left for this period of time. Other trees can be felled after about 20 years. They can be cut down so that side shoots sprout from the stump and this coppicing provides good poles for fencing within 7 years, as well as wood for fuel.

The young shoots, springing up from near ground level, need to be protected from animals, as do the young saplings which have to be planted to keep up the supply of wood and timber.

It came to be the custom that the lord should be allowed to fence his woodland for a period of 5 years or so to allow the trees to become established. But there are incidents of the fencing being pulled down by angry commoners when the lord tried to extend this period of enclosure. To avoid the need for fencing around a coppice of trees, it was possible to use an alternative method of producing small branches. This was to cut them from the tree at head height, a method called pollarding.

In hunting parks the trees were often pollarded and there the animals could be safely left to graze without damage to the young shoots. **(The legend of the oaks in Bradgate being 'beheaded' at the same time as Lady Jane Grey is not an absolutely improbably story. They would have been regularly pollarded).**

For woodland, therefore, fencing and enclosures are very important to protect trees. In the unenclosed 'waste' where timber might disappear piecemeal and where sheep and goats might roam uncontrolled to overgraze the land, woodland becomes non-viable and bracken and heather take hold. The temptation for a landowner to enclose and manage the 'waste' becomes strong: the urge to resist was obviously similarly strong from a community which depended on free grazing for its animals.

The law clearly stated that the lords of the manor could only

The Story of Charnwood and its Footpaths

enclose and cultivate portions of their land if they left sufficient common land for the rights of commoners.

Enclosure of common land was an important matter, dealt with in the high courts. Less serious matters of dispute were taken to Manorial courts and those concerning the management of the 'waste' were dealt with in the open air swanimote court (based on the Saxon 'Swainmotes'). Complaints of wood stealing, deer poaching, failure to repair the 'great Forest fence' or grazing more than a fair share of animals on the land were heard at these courts.

With this constant check on proper control of the common land the woodland of Charnwood remained viable for hundreds of years on the largely unenclosed 'waste', supporting livestock and providing wood. Early medieval enclosures were few and far between. For instance, in the flat land around Barrow, on the banks of the Soar, clearings were made for an early settlement at Quorn long before Domesday Book, and cultivation gradually extended westwards. There were three very early little monastic clearings at Ulverscroft (1134) and Charley (1190) and Alderman's Haw (1224) where monks cleared the 'waste' and farmed the land.

There was also land being cleared and farmed at Woodhouse (1228), Swithland (1199) and Woodthorpe (1236), Beaumanor (1277) and Maplewell (1284) but most other clearances and enclosures were confined to the periphery of the forest, on the sites of the earlier Saxon settlements.

From 1348 to 1390, when the Black Death cut down the population, the process of clearing the waste slowed down. And indeed, much of the cleared land must have fallen into decay, so extreme was the death toll among the population.

ANNO QUADRAGESIMO OCTAVO

GEORGII III. REGIS.

●●

Cap. 133.

An Act for allotting and inclosing the Foreſt or Chace of *Charnwood*, otherwiſe *Charley Foreſt* or *Chace*, and *Rothley Plain*, in the County of *Lei-ceſter*.   [18th June 1808.]

WHEREAS there are within the County of *Leiceſter* ſeveral large Tracts of Open Commonable Grounds or Waſte Lands, known by the Names of *The Foreſt* or *Chace of Charnwood* otherwiſe *Charley Foreſt* or *Chace*, and *Rothley Plain*, containing in the whole by Eſtimation, Eighteen thouſand Acres or thereabouts: And whereas the Soil of the ſaid Grounds and Lands, with other Rights in and over the ſame, is veſted, or reputed to be veſted, in the Lords or Owners of the ſeveral Manors, Lordſhips, Precincts, or Territories of *Grooby, Barrow, Whitwick, Loughborough, Beaumanor, Sheepſhead, Knight Thorpe, Thorpe Acre, Garendon, Gracedieu, Belton, Whitwick, Ulveſcroft, Charley, Bardon,* and *Thringſton*, all in the ſaid County of *Leiceſter*, or ſome of them; together with the Honourable *Auguſtus Richard Butler Danvers*, and *Peter Crompton* Eſquire, who are alſo or claim to be entitled to the Soil and other Rights in and over Parts of the ſaid Lands; and ſome other Perſons who claim to be entitled to the Soil of ſmall Portions thereof; and the reſpective Limits or Boundaries are for the moſt Part well known: And whereas the ſaid Lands lie or are reputed to lie within the ſeveral Pariſhes, Conſtableries, Townſhips, Hamlets, or Places of *Ratby, Newtown Linford, Bradgate, Holgate, Thurcaſton, Cropſton, Swithland, Barrow, Rothley, Woodhouſe Eaves, Woodthorpe, Beaumanor, Loughborough, Knight Thorpe, Garendon, Sheepſhead, Belton, Gracedieu, Swithland, Thringſton, Whitwick, Hugglescote,* and *Donington on the Heath, Stanton-under-Bardon, Markfield, Ulveſcroft, Charley,*

The Story of Charnwood and its Footpaths

There were no new villages founded in Charnwood until a much later date.

The manorial pattern of woodland management and farming in the small clearances set up in early medieval times, continued for six or seven hundred years despite fluctuations in population and changing needs of farming.

The great, dramatic changes came with the Enclosure Acts of 1808. Many of the effects on the agricultural economy and on the landscape of England, described in every social history textbook, are clearly visible in Charnwood.

The preamble to the Charnwood Enclosure award explains its intention:-

And whereas the said Open Commonable Grounds and Wast Lands lie in the Vicinity of several large manufacturing Towns, in nearly the centre of the Kingdom: and great parts thereof are in their present state of little or no Value, but capable, if enclosed, of affording, not only very great additional Pasturage, but also of producing great Quantities of Corn and Grain of all kinds: and it would be of great public utility as well as of great Benefit and Advantage to all persons interested in the said Grounds and Lands respectively if the same were inclosed, and allotted unto the several Persons interested therein; according to their several and respective Rights and Interests therein.

(Enclosure Act, 1808. Cap 133)

The landowners were in favour of enclosure and the Act became law; protests against the process did not prevail and the traditional pattern of land management changed dramatically within a very short space of time. Plots of land were allotted to those people who had rights of pasturage over the common. Free access to grazing over the whole area was exchanged for ownership of a plot of land. New landowners were obliged to fence or wall their plots, improve the drainage and pay for roads. It was an expensive business and the small plots were often not really viable and many small owners sold their plots to richer men, often the original lord of the manor. Thus, the biggest plots of land in the Charnwood area went to George Harry, Earl of Stamford (Groby), Thomas March Phillips Esq., (Shepshed), Rt. Hon. Francis Rawdon Hastings (Barrow, Whitwick and Loughborough) and Wm. Herrick Esq., (Beaumanor). Lesser folk received small plots in exchange for their rights of Common — and many must have felt they had received a very poor deal!

The impact of the Enclosures on the landscape was tremendous. The poet John Clare, writing about Enclosure in his part of Northamptonshire spoke for many when he lamented the loss of the wide open spaces, the parcelling of land into little pieces and the closure of paths with 'no road here' signs. When we survey the Charnwood landscape or when we browse through the Charnwood Enclosure Award maps (in Leicester Records Office) we can see what John Clare meant. We can see the geometrically shaped little fields and we look in vain for the ancient trackways which must have led to Ives Head and the old Swanimote rock from all the various settlements from which the commoners came to the swanimote courts.

It is unfortunate for us as walkers that the old tracks were not considered worthy of note by the Enclosure Award makers. Paths over enclosed land were generally recorded in that

The Story of Charnwood and its Footpaths

document mainly to establish the right of access of the new owners of the land to their fields. Traditional paths were not recorded, because it was not the purpose of the Award to do so. At this point, therefore, many paths were lost. Charnwood once had many more paths which must have crossed the land on quite major routes as well as many little tracks used for local purposes, such as herding and wood collecting.

This feature of the Enclosure Awards was pointed out as early as 1894 by Lord Eversley, a great campaigner for public access. He speaks of the loss of footpaths over land enclosed by Act of Parliament. **"In such case, if the Enclosure Award does not show the path it may be held that it did not exist at the date of the Award......although the path may have been continuously, largely and openly used, perhaps for a century."** He points out that most Rights of Way had arisen simply and solely from long continued use. It had never been the custom to make an *overt* act of dedication to creat a footpath: it just *was* one!

But without the necessary written evidence, the footpaths were vulnerable in the eyes of the law.

Tracks from the Swanimote rock to the Hermitage and across High Sharpley are now labelled 'Private' although long considered to be public rights of way by many people in the area. There is no footpath route from Longcliffe to the Outwoods or to Snell's Nook, although the 1911 L.F.A. book of walks was able to recommend a route 'whose publicity is not quite certain......indeed, in parts of it, it is quite certainly private. But it is allowed to pedestrians to use it if they are taking tea or refreshment at the cottage in Longcliffe Plantation or if a small fee is paid. The walk is to be recommended.' There is, alas, no-one now serving tea at 'Mr. Walker's cottage' and the lovely walk between high banks of rhododendron bushes and thence along an avenue of trees to the Golf House and the footpath along the 'Old Navigation' canal to Nanpantan is now denied us, and we have to walk along the busy, pavementless road.

To some extent, this deficiency of the Enclosure Acts has been remedied by later legislation and by generous 20th century gifts of land in Charnwood for public access. The situation today is not as bad as it was when J.B. Firth wrote his ***Highways and Byways in Leicestershire*** (1926):

"Of the choicest viewpoints scarcely one is open to the public as of right. The principal exception is the old Windmill summit at Woodhouse Eaves. Bardon Hill is private: so is the crest of the Warren Hills above the Copt Oak and Whitwick Road; and Broombriggs and Beacon Hills......are also closed, and the sacred birds of sport must never be disturbed. Practically speaking, therefore, Charnwood Forest, where for centuries the wayfarer might wander at will, has become a district without footpaths."......

The areas he mentions now have footpaths: and many are now public open spaces. Both these feature are due to the philanthropy, generosity and sheer hard work of Victorian Leicestershire men and women.

In his book ***Commons, Forests and Footpaths*** (1910) Lord Eversley outlines the history of the Commons and Footpaths society (founded in 1865) which strove to counteract the worst effects of the enclosure of common land. The first societies he describes are those in or near London, claiming right of access

The Story of Charnwood and its Footpaths

to the Commons of Wimbledon and Hampstead Heath: but here in Leicester we were quick to protest against the loss of access to footpaths which existed across our common land.

There is mention of a Leicestershire Footpath Society as early as the 1840s, though we do not know much about it. But by 1886 our records show that the present one was very actively taking action against landowners who prevented people walking on rights of way across their land.

One very early example of an incident of litigation over access is described in a very readable little history of the first 25 years of the Leicestershire Footpath Association, written by Harry Peach (a man famous in Leicester for his work with the Dryad art firm as well as for his footpath work).

He describes the incident "when Mr Napier Reeve, then Clerk to the Peace, threatened the Earl of Stamford, in an early attempt to close Bradgate Park, to break down his barriers on a certain date if they were not removed. The story goes on that the barriers were removed before Mr Reeve's arrival."

Later, after the formation of the present Leicestershire Footpath Association in 1886, many other respectable Leicester gentlefolk took up the battle cry sounded by Lord Eversley and the Commons Preservation Society.

These early stalwarts of Leicester, many of whose names are now lost and forgotten, made history by surveying footpaths, procuring evidence of past and present usage, marking them on maps, collecting public opinion regarding obstructions, discovering and publicising the law relating to footpaths, informing landowners of any infringement, requesting removal of obstacles and, when all else failed, organising 'mass trespass' to demand right of passage.

"*Let us appreciate the courtesy of the noble owner, by our courtesy and enjoy the Park as working gentlemen may do, as those who know 'that the greatest foe to liberty is he who abuses it'. So in our rambles over the Park, we will look out for the keeper, not to avoid him but to learn from him how we may avoid any trespass*".

W. Napier Reeve (Eliot Roscoe) *Bradgate Park*

There is a lovely story told by Harry Peach and recorded in the minutes of the L.F.A. of a dispute over glebe lands paths in Swithland; **"the vicar of Swithland at that time must have been rather a terror as there was continuous trouble about the Swithland path. On May 18th 1889 a party of ladies and gentlemen drove to Swithland and removed barriers at the end of the path"**.

On the whole, the L.F.A. avoided such drastic action. They were not so aggressively defensive of their rights as neighbouring Derbyshire and normally preferred to work by legal means.

By their persistence and meticulous attention to detail and to the law, the L.F.A. won many of their cases and by 1904 they had produced a footpath map of Leicestershire, based on the 1835, first edition, Ordnance Survey maps and the 1883 6" maps, with all the legally established footpaths and bridleways marked on it.

This map was accepted as legal evidence of the existence of rights of way when the Definitive Path survey was undertaken by the County in 1952: and at least one rambler of my acquaintance still uses his copy when walking in Charnwood today!

In 1894, mainly at Lord Eversley's insistence, clauses were inserted in the Local Government Act, declaring it to be the duty of District Councils, as Highway Authorities, to maintain public rights of way. This was in fact a tremendous step forward in the preservation of footpaths because the Councils have been able to record and signpost footpaths and to threaten litigation against transgressing landowners in a way that private citizens never could. If we now meet with an obstruction, we take our complaints to County Hall and expect action to be taken on our behalf.

A great deal has been achieved. The law is now established that no landowner may close or divert a footpath without going through the due process of law, which is an expensive and slow-moving business. Footpaths are now marked as rights of way on Ordnance Survey maps and Definitive maps are held at County Hall. The routes marked on them are legally enforceable.

But, as Lord Eversley himself remarked, **"much still remains to be done"**. Footpath associations still have to keep a sharp eye open for infringements of the law. They also have to take constant note of applications for diversions and closures of footpaths. Within recent times there has been a tremendous increase in the number of applications to quarry or extract minerals from land over which footpaths cross.

There has also been an increase in the number of applications from farmers. Pasture land has been increasingly ploughed for crops and, instead of rolling a pathway across the ploughed land to re-instate the path, as the law demands, many farmers have applied for diversion orders to require walkers to go round the edges of fields.

With the emphasis on 'agribusiness', however, there has been such a large scale removal of hedges (which are an obstacle to large combine harvesters) that walkers have become wary of allowing these 'edge of the field' diversions to be made. It seems safer to preserve the ancient and logical line from church spire to church spire, whenever practicable rather than accept a diversion round a hedgerow which can no longer be looked upon as a permanent field boundary.

The Story of Charnwood and its Footpaths

When the Leicestershire Footpath Association began, its aims were primarily to get footpaths legalised and its main work could be described as litigious. The rambling section was a later development which gradually became of equal importance to the 'pressure group' work.

Outings to the country, long fashionable for people of wealth and leisure, became increasingly important for poorer people in the 19th century. The period which gave us the Enclosure Acts also saw the growth of towns, of industry and transport and a corresponding demand for healthy outdoor activity for the poor townspeople.

Country walking became a popular, cheap recreation, as well as the usual form of transport to work.

As early as 1800, outings were being organised from Loughborough to the Charnwood beauty spots and by the 1920s various walking clubs were founded.

In the early 20th century, several philanthropic, wealthy gentlemen and women were moved to present or bequeath land as open spaces for public recreation. In Charnwood we have large tracts of lovely countryside donated to the people of Leicestershire. Bradgate Park, Beacon Hill, the Outwoods and Swithland Woods are probably the most well-known, but there are also many newer additions, like Jubilee Wood and Broombriggs and there are unpretentious little stretches of paths along old railway lines, like the recently dedicated one near Shepshed, by White Horse Wood, and picnic sites, and seats donated by or in memory of people who have loved Charnwood.

These gifts, particularly noticeable in the first few walks in this book and in the Way In from Loughborough, are now maintained and protected by the County Council.

It is the County Council's task, in conjunction with the parish councils, to preserve and maintain footpaths, on private land as well as on donated land. It also has to consider the requests of landowners to make changes on their land which might affect the rights of way across it, in the light of the needs of all the local interests involved.

It is a difficult task to balance the often conflicting interests of all those who wish to use Charnwood for agricultural or recreational purposes: and Governmental policies often confuse the issues even further. On big issues like roads or housing, 'national interest' overrides local protest, as it did in the building of the motorway through the Forest and in the quarrying of Buddon Wood.

The 20th century has increasingly seen the need for legislation to protect areas of natural beauty like Charnwood. As early as 1932 there were moves to establish the whole of Charnwood as a National Park but little came of them. Restrictions on building in the Forest followed the 1947 **Town and Country Planning Act**, but the demand for new housing is constantly nibbling away at the decision not to allow encroachment on the open spaces of Charnwood.

The National Parks and Access to the Countryside Act of 1949 was largely concerned with National Parks and areas designated as being of outstanding natural beauty. Although Charnwood is not designated as a National Park, walkers did benefit from the Act under its provisions for the making of access agreements or orders and the buying of land to enable the public to have access to 'open country' of moor, heath, downland and woodland, rivers and canals.

The Story of Charnwood and its Footpaths

It was this act which required County Councils to produce definitive maps in conjunction with the various parishes: and Leicestershire can take pride in the fact that it was particularly efficient in carrying out this requirement. Our maps were produced very promptly! and our county is now comparatively well-endowed with footpaths.

The Wild-life and Countryside Act of 1981 has not been an unqualified blessing for walkers, allowing as it does certain kinds of bulls to be kept in fields which have footpaths (previously an illegal practice in Leicestershire). The change of law has not affected walking in Charnwood as much as in other parts of Leicestershire as it is not primarily cattle country. The only bulls I have met on the walks in this book have been safely behind stone walls!

What is needed now, probably more than legislation, is education in care and concern for the countryside.

In some parts of Charnwood the land borders very closely on towns and new housing estates and it is very distressing to see the amount of vandalism and litter in these areas. It is equally distressing to see land privately owned and farmed with business efficiency by landowners with little respect for the lover of the countryside. Law-abiding footpath walkers are sometimes looked upon as potential hunt-saboteurs by farmers and landowners!

But some cheering moves have been made recently to encourage co-operation between various bodies using the countryside and, in the face of the terrible havoc wrought on Charnwood, it is reassuring to know that there is a growing awareness of the need to co-operate to protect the beautiful countryside which we have inherited.

The Country Landowners' Association has recently put forward a policy statement which makes encouraging remarks about co-operation with ramblers and the N.F.U. is similarly presenting a less aggressive face to walkers.

Leicestershire Rural Community Council recently organised a Day Conference on footpaths, called "Conflict or Co-operation?" and it is hoped to follow this up with a series of meetings to promote co-operation rather than conflict when those who make a living from the land meet people who use it primarily for recreation.

Leicestershire Environmental Forum organises walks and talks by farmers, landowners and rambling associations and others who are then able to show the general public their particular concerns in the way the countryside is used or abused.

Educational establishments, field centres and nature trails are providing services to enable children and adults to understand and appreciate the countryside; and there are lectures and classes for subjects like bird-watching, geology, landscape history, botany and other such topics which the true rambler becomes interested in.

It is good to know that there are people determined to protect and preserve all which makes the land lovely and varied and to encourage understanding and appreciation of country matters. All praise is due to those who have worked, and who are working, to acquire more access to beauty spots, to enable walkers to escape from busy roads and travel along the ancient trackways which enable us to enjoy the beauty of the English countryside so close to our towns and cities!

And long may the process continue!

Heather MacDermid. 1985.   Now Walk On......

Bradgate Park

Beginners to Bradgate tend to collect just outside the main gates entrance in the wall of the park, at Newtown Linford.

On my first visit to Leicester I was taken by friends to Bradgate. We walked 100 yards, deposited babies and picnic basket on a rug and admired the River Lin, the deer, the old oaks and the rocks of the hills beside the drive. We watched the people walking by on the road (closed to traffic, as it was not a Thursday) and idly wondered where they, unencumbered by babies, were going. As our children grew older we explored the hills beside the main drive and we played hide and seek in the hollow oak trees.

We took grandparents and push chairs along to the ruins of Bradgate House, read the notice which told us that Mr. Bennion had donated this park for the enjoyment of the People of Leicestershire, we saw where the deer fed and we played Cowboys and Indians on the rocky outcrop near the ruins, all within sight of the main track.

Our first visit to Old John was from Hunts Hill car park. It was years before I crossed the area between, possibly after I joined a walking club and discovered that there were maps which helped you find your way across the Great Outdoors! And even now I feel a slight sense of adventure as I cross those bracken tracks not marked with a dotted green line on the Ordnance Survey maps!

Now, my favourite route to introduce visitors to Bradgate is to go up to Tyburn from Newtown Linford church and along the ridge to Old John keeping to the high ground to admire the view, and then through Swithland Wood and back on the lower route via the main drive from Hallgates, past Cropston Reservoir and Bradgate House.

As you walk along the ridge from Tyburn to Old John you will be walking due north, with a panoramic view of Charnwood to your left and views of the beautiful deer park of Bradgate stretching out below you on your right.

As you climb up onto the rocky outcrops of the War Memorial you can stop and survey the skyline of Charnwood landmarks. One can pick out Groby, to whose manor this deer park belonged, and Markfield with its church spire and distinctive rocks, and Copt Oak, easily recognised by its twin radio masts. The wooded hills of Bardon, Timberwood and Birch Hill stand out on the horizon and are to be visited in later walks in this book. From these places you will be able to look back to this Tyburn-to-Old-John ridge with a pleasing sense of familiarity as you recognise the outline of this saddleback (even when you cannot actually pick out Old John itself, hidden as it often is by its rocks and trees.)

Between you and the skyline of wooded hills you have a good 'map's eye view' of Blakeshay wood and Benscliffe wood (which have, alas, no public paths through them) and to the north west you can see Broombriggs Hill and Beacon Hill beyond (both completely open to the public).

The flat plain to be seen to the north, through the gap in the hills, is Loughborough.

From the War Memorial you can look down on the ruins of Bradgate House, (which cannot be seen from Old John itself) nestling beside Bowling Green spinney, on your right. This great brick house was built for the Greys of Groby in 1490 and it is pleasant to stand here and think of Lady Jane Grey at home, reading, while her family and friends were up here, hunting.

"No need to ask whither, where does Leicester spend its holiday but at Bradgate Park".

W. Napier Reeve (Eliot Roscoe) *Bradgate Park: its story and its scenery.* 1849

Old John Bradgate

Bradgate Park

Whatever we feel about hunting, we can still catch an idea of the grandeur of these deer parks as we see the herd of deer feeding down by the river or grazing in small groups in quiet, unexpected places. And we can get our excitement taking aim with our cameras to take our good 'shots' home with us.

It is salutary to look over to Bardon, once the neighbouring deer-park, and to give thanks that Bradgate has been preserved from the ravages of quarrying and conifer tree planting that have ruined that once beautiful park.

Between the War Memorial and Old John is a lovely enclosed spinney, where deer often graze, and just outside its walls is a brick and stone walled enclosure built onto the rock face, which was formerly a stable for horses used by the 7th Lord Stamford when racing around the park.

The distinctive beer-mug shaped folly of Old John is an 18th century construction built on the site of an old mill. The story is that old John, a retainer of the Greys, was killed by a falling maypole in 1786 at a coming of age party for one of the Earl of Stamford's family. This marks the highest point of the park and provides a marvellous viewing place. The toposcope, erected by people of Newtown Linford in 1953, indicates landmarks to be seen, like Nottingham castle, Buddon Wood, Billesdon Coplow and Belvoir and by looking at these distant hills you realise that this must have been a landmark for long distance prehistoric hill routes.

You can also see Leicester cathedral and realise, with surprise, that you are only 5 miles as the crow flies from the heart of the city.

You need to leave the high ground, (where people collect to admire the view, to boast that they've been right to the top, to fly their model aeroplanes or ride their sledges and try out their skis in winter) and move from the security of the park to venture out to Swithland woods, a couple of fields outside the park walls!

The walk through Swithland Woods is a popular family outing and there is no real danger of getting lost. If you keep to the highest ground as you walk east through the woods you will be able to see the fenced-off, water-filled old quarries. You can look over the fencing and see the rocks on the far side of the quarry where the inscription, reflected in the water, tells you that the woods were donated by the Rotary Club of Leicester. The quarries were worked until Victorian times, producing the famous Swithland slate.

When you return to Newtown Linford you can admire the church's Swithland slate roof and the beautifully inscribed headstones in the churchyard. Most people are also interested to see the 'apprentice's gravestone' which used to stand in the graveyard but which is now, for safe keeping, inside the church. It has curiosity value because, although made up entirely of sample lettering, it was apparently chosen, and used, as a legitimate headstone!

Marion's Cottage, close to the park entrance, is now an information centre for the park, the wild life and the rocks of Charnwood. It is possible to find out, from the displays or from the books on sale, details about Bradgate House and the Grey family, who became Earls of Stamford and owned the park until it was brought by Charles Bennion and bequeathed to the City and County of Leicester on December 29th 1928.

Bradgate Park

As you walk through the main drive of the park you will walk beside Cropston reservoir and past the site of the lost village of Bradgate, which was allowed to fall into decay when the great house was built. The house itself was the home of Lady Jane Grey when she was called upon to become Queen of England after the death of Edward VI, Henry VIII's only male heir. She was queen for a mere nine days, in 1553, and as you walk through the park you will see the ancient hollow pollarded oak trees which were reputedly 'beheaded' when she was, as a token of mourning for the young queen.

The ruins and grounds of the house are open in summer months and it is possible to admire the fine fish pond and the jousting area and to enter the chapel to see the tombs of Henry Grey, 1st Earl of Stamford and Anne Burleigh, his wife.

Your route back to Newtown Linford follows the beautiful little river Lin with its five pools and little waterfalls. This is a lovely place to loiter before returning to the refreshment stops beyond the car park of Newtown Linford.

"No Leicester man but what goes to Bradgate, no one who goes to Bradgate but what climbs the hill to Old John".

    W. Napier Reeve (Eliot Roscoe) *Bradgate Park; its story and its scenery. 1849*

Introductory Walk Around Bradgate Park

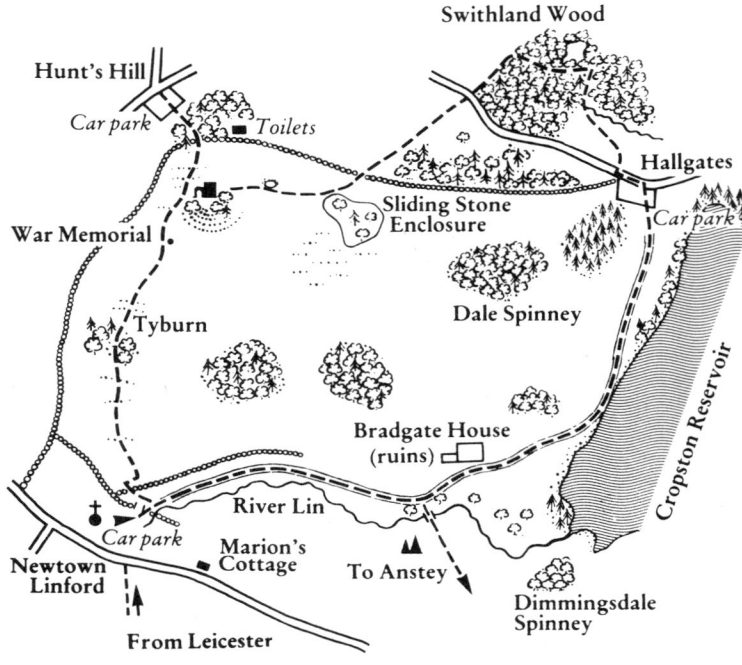

BRADGATE PARK, SWITHLAND WOODS, HALLGATES AND CROPSTON RESERVOIR. (4 MILES)

From **Newtown Linford,** make your way through the car-park by the church to the main park gates. Go through the high kissing gate in the park wall, just to the right of the main gates, and turn left. Cross the main drive and follow the gravel track, with the park wall on your left. This track joins the bridle way and curves round to the right, passing through a wide gateway in the wall.

The clump of trees on the hill ahead of you is **Tyburn**, your first goal. Take any of the good tracks up to it. (My favourite is to turn right and walk close to the wall on my right for about 80 yards and then turn left, up the first good clear track through the bracken.)

Walk through, or beside, the Tyburn spinney and continue in the same direction uphill to the **War Memorial** and then on to the **Old John spinney** enclosure. **Old John** itself is just on the other side of this walled enclosure. On the far side of Old John is a useful toposcope, indicating places which can

Introductory Walk Around Bradgate Park

be seen on a fine day. The direction you need is nearly due East, towards Rothley. Go steeply downhill, past a little circular pond, towards the left of a squat, square Water works building.

Before you reach the water works building you will meet the wall of **Sliding Stone Enclosure** and a few yards further on you need to fork left downhill to meet the park wall at a big gate, to the left of the water works building.

Go through the high kissing gate in the park wall and continue (in the same direction) down a tree-lined drive, passing the water works building on your right and keeping the hedge on your right for two fields, until you meet the Cropston to Shepshed road, at the footpath sign.

A track immediately opposite continues in the same direction for two fields keeping just to the west of **Swithland Woods,** but the prettier route is to go through the little gap in the stone wall a few yards to your right and to follow the path which takes you inside the wood. Keep close to the wall on your left to follow the western edge until you reach the point where the path from the outside edge of the wood turns into the wood, just below the wooden chalets, at a post and rail fence.

Here the path takes a sharp right turn and goes east through the woods until you meet the main (North-South) drive through the wood, which takes you back to Bradgate.

(If you wish to see the quarries you need to keep to the high ground, where you will soon see the high fence which surrounds them.)

Turn right along the main drive, which passes close to the quarries, and walk south towards Bradgate.

When the path widens into a big bridge crossing a tiny stream, turn left along the edge of the wood with the stream on your right for about 100 yards and then cross the plank bridge over the stream, leaving the wood and walking diagonally across a wide, open meadow between the wood on your left and a line of trees and the road on your right.

Meet the road at a gate beside Horseshoe Cottage, and turn left along the road for a short distance (round a dangerous corner.) **Hallgates Car park** is on your right. Pass through the car park to enter Bradgate Park by the gate in the park wall and continue along the main drive to **Bradgate House**, beside **Cropston Reservoir**.

From Bradgate House, the main drive follows the River Lin to the starting point of Newtown Linford.

Walk 1

Introduction

This walk can be started from Newtown Linford, as in the introductory walk, going to Old John and then swinging left down to Hunt's Hill car park. If you have a car, you may prefer to shorten the walk by omitting the route through the park and start from the car park at Hunt's Hill.

From Hunt's Hill you will be walking down a hill with lovely views over the golf course by Spring Hill Wood towards Maplewell and Woodhouse Eaves. There are lots of tempting 'side attractions' here with places to loiter in and to explore. Broombriggs Farm, which is now an amenity centre with a farm trail and information about how a farm works, is just to the left of the road as you walk into Woodhouse Eaves, and Windmill Hill is only a little way further along the road.

Anyone weary at this point could be left to explore these delights and to enjoy some refreshment in the village, while you continue on your route. (You might need to arrange to meet them later with the car or agree to take a bus back to Leicester!).

I personally prefer to decide in advance whether I'm going to make it a 'stopping-to-look' walk or a 'covering-the-ground' walk, as I find it tiring to mix the two. Visits to places of interest usually tire me more than the walks do! But it's nice to have the choice: and it IS possible to combine them.

Woodhouse Eaves is a very attractive place to stop. The pubs and restaurants are very welcoming and there are shops and toilets. There is even a bookshop which sells coffee, and a car park.

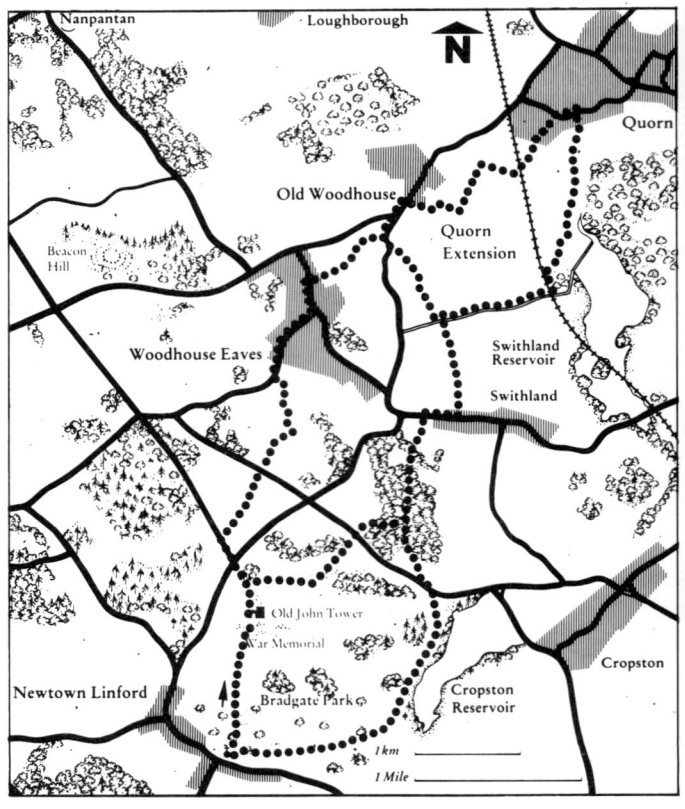

Walk 1 - Branching Out From Bradgate

Woodhouse Eaves, a daughter village of Old Woodhouse, expanded after the Enclosures and did not have its own church until 1837. The building, designed by William Railton, sits on top of an old quarry! Before it was built, villagers from Woodhouse Eaves used to have to go to Old Woodhouse church and the path that we now take has been properly surfaced for many years to enable churchgoers to walk cleanly between the two villages.

Old Woodhouse is a very pretty village. On the outskirts you pass Pestilence Cottage, built for the Rawlins family to commemorate their escape from the ravages of the Great Plague in London, 1665.

The church stands at a road junction at one end of the village. It is rather a strange Victorian building, reconstructed in 1878 on an old site. It has a squat slate roof and a tall chimney! Inside are memorials to the Herrick family who owned Beaumanor from the 17th century until 1925. The village houses look very old because they are built in local stone and slate, but are actually dated 1856! The Herrick family replaced their old cottages in Victorian times with these 'little ornamental cottages with porches and gables'.

The area between Woodhouse and Swithland is rather flat, and Rushey Fields farm is an example of bare and functional modern farm buildings with tall metal silos. There is, therefore, an incentive to choose the alternative extension in Quorn, which is a more attractive route. Quorn village itself is well worth a trip for those interested in fine brick houses (on the side road, and not seen if you hurtle through on the main A6).

Our path turns off before the centre of the village is reached and goes to the old mill. This is a very pleasant place to loiter. Children often play in the stream and Buddon Wood, on the far side of the stream looks peaceful still, although one can hear the A6 road and the occasional rumbling of quarry machinery behind the screen of trees.

You will pass very close to the landscaped gardens of the Victorian reservoir of Swithland. (Victorian reservoirs were constructed on the PRIVATE NO ENTRY principle and so you can only admire the water gardens through the dark, forbidding rails.) If you wish to see the reservoir itself you must leave the route for a short distance, turning left along the lane across the railway, and then return. An added attraction is the old Great Central Railway line, which has now been restored for stream train journeys between Rothley and Loughborough. At weekends you may see the trains chuffing along very merrily. (The railway line actually crosses the reservoir on a very impressive viaduct. It is worth the detour to see it. The reservoir is a haven for water birds of all kinds).

The path I describe does not enable you to see much of Swithland itself. It is a very long, strung-out village with the church and pub at the far end. If one takes the path that leads to the church end of the village, one is faced with a long road walk to Swithland woods. For that reason, I have described the path from Rushall Field farm to Swithland woods.

It is possible to catch buses from Swithland and the Griffin pub can be recommended as a place to wait, if you decide to shorten the walk! The main road through the village may be long but it is not unattractive!

Pestilence Cottage Old Woodhouse

Walk 1 - Branching Out From Bradgate

Our path back to Bradgate goes through Swithland Woods, passing close to the old quarry pool. If you climb up the bank you have lovely views of the steep rocky sides of the deep greeny-blue water, and you can read the inscription on the rocks which informs you that these woods were donated by the Rotary Club.

From this point you can choose to swing right, to return to Old John and Hunt's Hill car park or to swing left to Hallgates entrance to the park, where you can walk along the main drive, past Bradgate House, to Newtown Linford.

From Hunt's Hill	a 5 mile tour, excluding Quorn mill
	a 7 mile tour with the Quorn extension
From Newtown Linford	about 8 miles, excluding Quorn mill
	about 10 or 11 miles with the Quorn extension

The Wildlife and Countryside Act

Ploughing
Footpaths and bridleways which cross fields can be ploughed along with the remainder of the field provided that the path is restored within two weeks of the start of ploughing, or if prevented by exceptional weather conditions, as soon as practicable. Failure to restore the right of way is a criminal offence. Generally, footpaths or bridleways may not be ploughed where they pass along the edges of fields or headlands, and to do so where there is no right to plough is a criminal offence. Other public rights of way may not be ploughed wherever they are located, again unless there is a right to plough. Parish Councils are empowered to bring proceedings in respect of alleged ploughing offences on footpaths and bridleways.

Bulls
A bull may now be kept in a field containing a public path, bridleway or byway open to all traffic if it is under 10 months old or is not of a recognised dairy breed and is being run with cows or heifers. The recognised dairy breeds are British Friesian, British Holstein, Ayrshire, Dairy Shorthorn, Jersey, Guernsey and Kerry.

Dogs
The Dogs (Protection of Livestock) Act 1953 has been amended to make it an offence for a dog to be at large, which is otherwise than on a lead or under close control, in a field containing sheep. This law does not apply to the occupier's dogs, sheep dogs, police dogs, guide or working gun dogs, or packs of hounds.

Walk 1. Branching out from Bradgate

NEWTON LINFORD - OLD JOHN - WOODHOUSE EAVES - (EXTENSION TO QUORN) - SWITHLAND - SWITHLAND WOODS - BRADGATE (8 MILES)(START FROM HUNT'S HILL 6 MILES. EXTENSION TO QUORN 3 MILES)

From Newton Linford make your way through the park to Hunt's Hill car park. The quickest and prettiest route is to enter the park gates at Newtown Linford and turn left, following the park wall for a short distance. Go through the wall facing you and make your way uphill to **Tyburn,** the small grove of trees which is directly in line with **Old John** and the war memorial. Pass both these landmarks, admiring the views on all sides, and go downhill to the park gates in the left corner, past the toilets and through Hunt's Hill car park to the road beyond.

From Hunt's Hill car park - cross the Swithland-Newton Linford road and walk along the road signposted "Shepshed 6" for 300 yards. Turn right at the first gate (by a footpath sign) and walk with the hedge on your right. This field is very long, and drops steeply down, past a circular outcrop of rocky ground between you and a walled plantation on your left. The path should cross the field to the bottom left corner but if a good headland has been left it is easier to go round the edge of the field to this point.

The wooded hill straight ahead of you is Spring Hill wood, which borders the golf course you are about to cross.

Cross the stile in the corner of the field by the walled plantation and go down the narrow path between hedge on left and fence on right, straight down to the road. Cross straight over to the stile and slate bridge (by the footpath sign to Woodhouse Eaves) onto the golf course. The path is well signposted over the golf course and you should actually be aiming in a straight line for the hedge on the far side of the course, but just in case you are distracted by flying golf balls and the beautiful landscape gardening, I'll give the details......

Begin with the fence, hedge and young birch trees on your right, and pass the clubhouse which is some way over to your left. When you reach the tee in

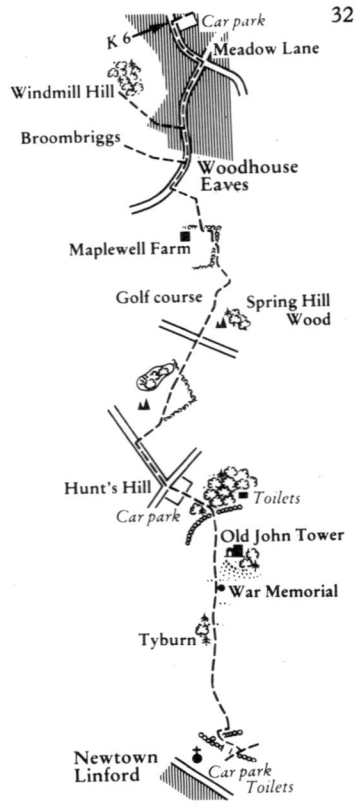

Walk 1 - Branching Out From Bradgate

the top corner, with **Spring Hill wood** on your right, go through the gap, drop down and continue across a fairway to meet a short stretch of hedge on your left. When this ends, turn right along the hedge facing you. When it ends, swing left, passing a clump of trees on your right, and cross a second fairway.

Once again, join a hedge on your left and cross to the wall opposite. Turn right and walk with the hedge on your left until you see 100 yards ahead of you the raised bank of a stream between you and the end of the golf course.

On your left is a stile into a field with **Maplewell Farm** in the far corner.

The path formerly went diagonally across to a gate at the right of the farm -but it is now correct to go right and follow the hedge round to this point, to avoid crops.

Go through the gateway to follow the track with the hedge on your left, pass the stables and garage of the house and follow the drive as it swings left, round the house onto Maplewell Road.

Turn right and walk down the road to **Woodhouse Eaves.** Turn left at the

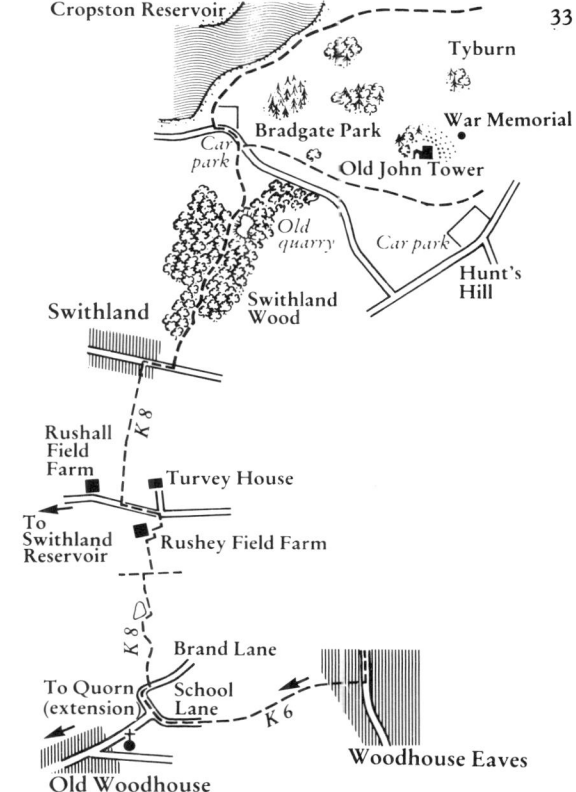

Walk 1. Branching out from Bradgate

staggered crossroads.

(**From the crossroads in Woodhouse Eaves it is possible to go straight down Meadow Road along the K7 path to Rushey Fields farm, but the prettier route starts from further left along the village street, towards Quorn, and follows the old paved route to Woodhouse.**)

CHARNWOOD CIRCUIT, continued from page 52.

At the recreation ground carpark, in Woodhouse Eaves opposite the imposing red brick Wesleyan Methodist Chapel, follow the tarmac strip past the sports fields, keeping close to the wall and hedge on your left until you reach the Water Board railings. Cross the stile on your left and cut across the corner of the field to where the hedge juts out. Here you join the stream and walk with it on your right, through a tree lined path, to join School Lane, *Woodhouse*, at Lane End Cottage.

This charming lane meets Brand Lane near the derestriction sign. **If you wish to omit the Quorn extension and go straight to Rushey Fields farm, turn right from School Lane, Woodhouse, along Brand Lane. The K8 footpath leaves the road at a sharp bend, just past a white gate on the left. A good stile leads you into the field next to the white gate. Walk with the hedge on your left towards the silos of Rushey Fields farm. Cross the footbridge over the stream and join the concrete farm drive. Just before the farm buildings go through the fence on the right and pass to the right of the farm and cottages onto the lane. Turn left, passing Turvey house on your right.**

The Quorn extension rejoins the route here. (see page 38.)

The Quorn Extension

THE QUORN EXTENSION (from Old Woodhouse to Rabbits Bridge and Rushey Fields farm)

From School Lane, Woodhouse, turn left to *Old Woodhouse church,* pass Pestilence Cottage on your left and continue through the village.

Turn right at *Vicary Lane* and walk along the tarmac drive. Turn left at the junction, signposted to Well House, and follow the path round as it swings right. At the end of the first field the path turns left, where it meets the 'Private Road' sign. You are now walking towards the flat Loughborough plain. The Carillon Tower is visible in front of you.

When the drive bends right, at Well House, go straight on across the field towards Highfields farm. Before you reach the farm, turn right to join a hedge which is on the right. Walk with this hedge on your right, towards Buddon Wood, Mountsorrel Quarry and *the Great Central railway line.*

Turn left under the railway bridge and follow the green lane which moves gradually away from the railway line. When the lane opens up, swing left to cut across the corner of the field to

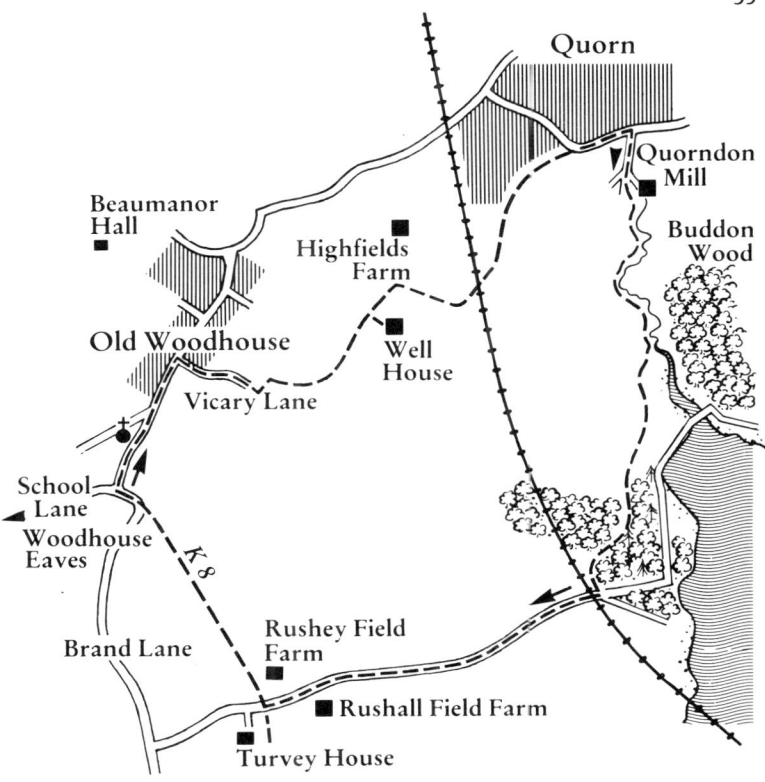

The Viaduct Swithland Reservoir

The Quorn Extension - Omit this page if you do not wish to go to Quorn

join the unadopted road which leads into Chaveney Road, *Quorn*.

Continue along the main road into Quorn for 150 yards and turn right at the F.P. sign opposite no. 21. Go through the wide gateway which leads to *Quorndon Mill*. When the drive swings left to cross the brick bridge over the brook go straight ahead through a series of green metal gates and walk beside the meandering stream on your left.

When the stream bends left, keep straight on, near the fence on the right. Go through the gate at the corner of the field and walk in the same direction with the hedge on your left.

At the end of the field where dark trees block your way, a footbridge leads you across the stream and sharp right, round the railings of the beautifully landscaped but very private water gardens of the Severn Trent Water Authority. Walk beside the railings and enjoy the tantalising glimpses! A footbridge leads you into an open field, where you move right to meet the railway line in the far corner. Walk beside the railway line in the next field.

Turn right at the lane onto the railway bridge and watch for the steam trains to go by (at weekends only!) (Go left along the lane if you wish to see *Swithland reservoir* - and then return).

To rejoin the route from Woodhouse, continue over the railway bridge and along the lane for half a mile until you pass *Rushall Field farm*, the first farmhouse, on your left. You need to walk 100 yards to find the fence beside the gate on your left which will take you to Swithland.

Walk 1 - Branching out from Bradgate

From the Swithland reservoir lane you need to turn off, to reach Swithland, when you are opposite Rushey Fields farm, with its 3 houses and huge metal silos.

The fence to cross is beside a metal farm gate. It is not signposted but can be found exactly mid-way between the imposing stone farmhouse of Rushall Field farm and Turvey House (at the end of a private little drive opposite the entrance to Rushey Fields farm).

Walk with the hedge on your left, crossing a fence halfway down the field. As you descend you should see a prominent straight hedge down the hillside facing you (a little on your right). At the bottom end of this hedge there is a concrete footbridge which you have to find by crossing the rough ground at the bottom of the field you are now in.

Pass over the bridge and keep the marker hedge on your left for two fields, one uphill and one down, until you reach the main street in *Swithland*. The stile is just to the right of the house (formerly it went through the garden).

Swithland is a long, strung-out village with very few facilities for a tired, hungry or thirsty walker. The Griffin Inn is a mile away to the left along the road. The road is pretty with lovely houses and gardens and some tempting-looking bus stops, but it would be a pity to miss the next section of the walk, through Swithland woods and Bradgate.

Turn right along the road until you reach the de-restriction sign. Turn left up a path between hedges beside a slate house. This track leads you straight into *Swithland woods.*

If you keep in a southerly direction walking on the main path or following the yellow markers of the bridle route you will come to the famous old slate quarries.

Pass the slate quarries and continue in the same direction, to reach the main road which passes the *Hallgate entrance* to Bradgate Park. You can swing left just before you reach the road, walking diagonally over the last field, to meet the road near the car park entrance. You can then walk through Hallgates carpark and along the main drive through the park to *Newtown Linford*.

If you wish to return to Hunts Hill car park from Swithland quarries pool, turn right by the fencing to pass the pool of the quarry on your right and keep due west on any of the little paths that follow the high ground, until you emerge from the wood. Turn left and walk with the wood on your left until you meet the road.

The footpath to Old John is directly opposite and Old John is clearly visible. Walk up the path to the park gates and turn right, beside the park wall. At the next park gates, just beyond Old John, turn right, past the toilets, to Hunts Hill car park.

Walk 2 - The Heart of the Forest

Introduction

For the first part of this walk it is easy to imagine yourself as a villager from Newtown Linford in times gone by, walking across the fields to the old mill by the stream and beyond that to the Priory of Ulverscroft.

The ruins of the priory are a picturesque reminder of a bygone age and at the beginning of this century they must have been a popular visiting place as there was a small museum and teas were served there. This was indeed one of the earliest enclosures of the forest. The priory was founded by Robert Bossu, second Earl of Leicester in 1134, for the Augustinian Eremites. It was only a small foundation for a few inmates and it was dissolved in 1539 but during the time the monks farmed it a large area of the forest was cleared. The wild areas provided the prior with marvellous hunting and hawking grounds. The priory is now the finest monastic ruin in Leicestershire and is scheduled as an ancient monument. The old prior's lodging is incorporated in the building.

The next landmark is Bawdon Castle. There is only a farm here and a walled rocky plantation with a commanding view. This, presumably, is 'Baldwyn's Castell' mentioned in old documents as a place in the forest. From Bawdon Castle there are marvellous panoramic views across the valley to Beacon Hill and Broombriggs Hill on your right and to Mt. St. Bernard's Abbey ahead and to the twin radio masts of Copt Oak. These are the most easily recognisable landmarks. Those with a good map or a good knowledge of the area will be able to point out many more beauty spots from this vantage point.

At the foot of the hill our route passes the former Charley

1km
1 Mile

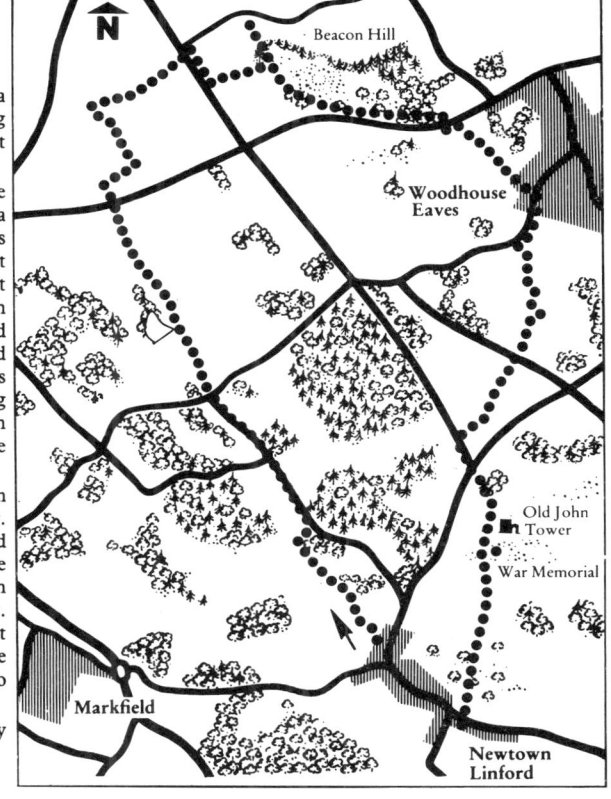

Ulverscroft Priory

Walk 2 - The Heart of the Forest

Introduction

Chapel. There are many of these little non-conformist chapels in the forest. This old Methodist chapel has now been converted into a modern house.

The name 'Charley' occurs frequently in this part of Charnwood. It is the name of the whole area and is the first clearing of the forest named in Domesday Book.

Our route goes next to Beacon Hill, passing very close to another ancient religious foundation, Alderman's Haw. Now an unpretentious farmhouse, nestling in the valley, it was once a hermitage with three resident monks, founded as an outpost cell of the priory of Bermondsey in Southwark in 1224. At the dissolution of the priory in the 14th century the land went to Thomas Farnham and the deeds are still held at Quorn House.

The whole of this area is steeped in history and spectacular in its views, as you cross from one ancient settlement to another. Beacon Hill is probably the most impressive but the view of the whole range of hills from Beacon and Broombriggs visible from Bawdon Castle is splendid.

Beacon Hill itself was probably a Bronze Age settlement. (Bronze Age relics were discovered there in 1858). Roman coins were found at the foot of the hill. From the top of the hill it is easy to see why ancient tribes would choose to build their earthworks there.

The whole of the hill was a gift to the County Council in 1947. Sixty-one acres of land were donated by A.J. Gimson (the first secretary of the Leicestershire Footpath Association) and A.V. Billson, and now stand as a lovely memorial to benefactors of the city. From the summit you are 818 ft. above sea level. There is a useful direction indicator to help you recognise the landmarks you can see.

The path which takes you up to the Beacon was donated by a subscription raised by the Leicestershire Footpath Association as a tribute to the work of their chairman, W.H. Rippin.

A similar path from Dean's Lane was dedicated as a celebration of the Queen's Silver Jubilee (1977).

Beacon Hill forms the halfway point in our heart-shaped walk. From here you go downhill (to Woodhouse Eaves, if you wish) or via Broombriggs Farm (which has a very interesting Farm Trail) or via Windmill Hill, which no longer has a windmill, but has a fine view from the top.

The route then covers the same ground as Walk 1, but in the opposite direction, back to Old John. (Top marks to those who can do it from memory! Instructions for those who think as I do, that it looks quite different this way!)

A lovely 10 mile day out in any season of the year.

The Charnwood Circuit described on page 46. connects walks 2 and 3 and leads from Ulverscroft Priory through Poultney Wood to Copt Oak. On this stretch of walk one gets impressive views over Charnwood, especially from the top of the hill near Whitcroft's Lane, beside the Nature Reserve. The very beautiful woodland here is unfortunately restricted to members of the Leicestershire Trust and so it is not possible to see the high rocks that the trees conceal.

The radio masts which are such a conspicuous feature of the Charnwood landscape relay radio and television signals and were moved from Bardon Hill when the quarrying interfered with reception.

Walk 2 - The Heart of the Forest

NEWTON LINFORD CIRCULAR VIA ULVERSCROFT PRIORY, BAWDON CASTLE, CHARLEY CHAPEL, WOODHOUSE EAVES, WINDMILL HILL, MAPLEWELL GOLF COURSE AND HUNTS HILL. (10 MILES)

Newtown Linford is a good starting point as it is a pretty village with good parking facilities and shops and loos.

The walk starts from the Markfield end of the village and is now well waymarked. Continue along the main village street towards Ulverscroft for 150 yards, then turn left opposite Johnscliffe Hotel down a track between houses. Cross the stile at the bottom into a narrow neck of field between hedge and stream. Keep in the same direction when the field widens out, moving slightly left to a stile beside a small oak tree in a hedge opposite. Bear slightly left across the third field to cross a footbridge.

Turn left along a track that runs from Ulverscroft Lane to John's Lee Wood. Pass the old ***Ulverscroft mill*** on your right, go through the gate and then turn right immediately to go uphill close to the mill. In the next field bear left down to the stream. In the far corner cross the footbridge and the stile beside the gate opposite. Now keep the stream on your left and make for a wooden fence in the corner of the field.

The next stile is halfway between the stream and the top corner of the field, and from here you keep close to the hedge on your right until, at the end of the field, you come to a lane which leads up to Ulverscroft Lane on your right.

Turn left along the lane for three quarters of a mile, passing the end of Polly Botts Lane. At the next T junction go straight over the road, through the gate opposite and follow the farm track that leads past ***Ulverscroft Priory***.

At the next farm gate and stile you can decide whether to follow the long Charnwood circuit route by keeping close to the wall on your left or to continue this walk by following the farm track to Ulverscroft Lodge.

(THE CHARNWOOD CIRCUIT CONTINUES ON PAGE 46)

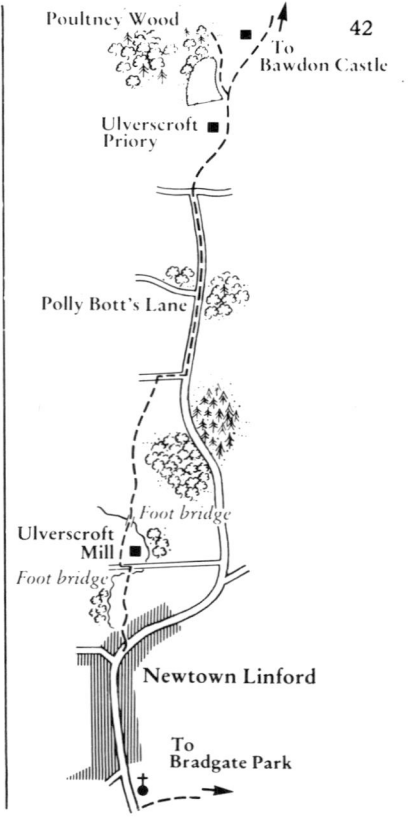

Walk 2 - The Heart of the Forest

From Ulverscroft Priory to Bawdon Castle.

To continue to Bawdon castle farm and Beacon Hill take the right fork of the track and pass to the right of *Ulverscroft Lodge* farm.

Pass between the farm buildings on your left and the stream on your right and continue in the same direction with the stream ditch on your right. Make for the gate straight ahead in the gap in the trees. The next field is a long narrow one. Go through the gate at the top and bear towards the right hand hedge until you come out on the Woodhouse to Copt Oak road at the top corner of the field.

Cross the stile on the opposite side of the road and continue for one field with the hedge on your right. In the corner, cross the stile on your right and immediately the one on your left. The path turns a right angle up to *Bawdon Castle farm* and you walk with the wall on your right for two fields, to join the farm road. Turn left here and follow the farm road into the (rough and muddy) field. Follow the wall on your right until it bends away from you and then swing left to cut across the corner and walk along the bottom hedge of the same field.

Keep the hedge and wall on your right. Pass a little old quarry and a walled plantation and a gate on your right. You can go through this gate and follow the wall of the plantation on your right, though the correct route is a little further down over a stile and back up to the plantation wall. Go downhill, skirting the plantation, to Charley Chapel. This is a small isolated Methodist Chapel dated 1862, now modernised as a house.

Cross the road and the stile to the left of the chapel and go down the field with the hedge on your right. Keep in the same direction, but walk with the next hedge on your left, by going through the gate and turning right through the gate facing you. Turn left and with the hedge on your left cross a small stream and meet the Cropston to Shepshed road opposite *Dean's Lane*.

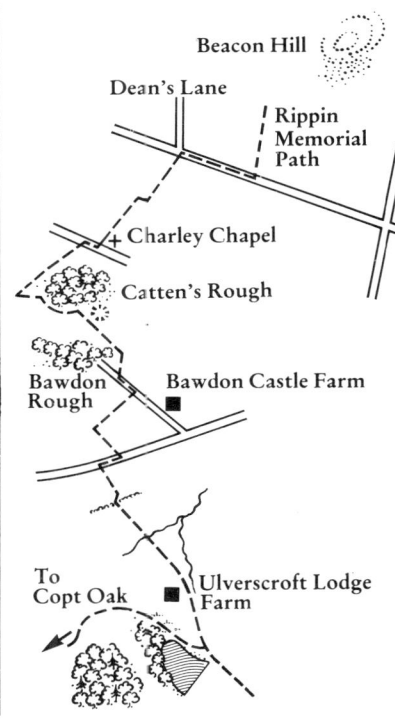

Walk 2 - The Heart of the Forest

From Dean's Lane to Maplewell Road

To approach **Beacon Hill** walk up Dean's Lane for three fields and turn right at the F.P. sign. Go through the iron kissing gate and walk along the Jubilee path which goes through a long narrow spinney of well established mixed beech, oak and holly trees. This path meets the Rippin Memorial path of more recently planted trees and both paths continue to Beacon Hill.

When the avenue of trees ends you will see the Beacon rocks in front of you through an opening in the wall on your left.

You can turn right and follow this wall along a good track to Beacon Hill car park and then swing left to the toposcope: but a more exciting route is to go straight for the rock face and go up and over the rocks, making for the trig. point. Go through one of the narrow gaps in the wall and scramble up the rocks of the 'devil's profile.'

Admire the views all round you and then continue along the high ground to reach the toposcope, which identifies for you the places to be seen.

Beacon Hill (802 feet)

Breedon 8¼
Ives Head 2½
High Sharpley 4
Mt St Bernard's 3¼
Timberwood Hill 2½ miles *due west*
Bardon 3
Copt Oak 2
Old John 2½ miles *south east*
Leicester 8
Billesdon 14 miles *due east*
Burrough Hill 16
Buddon 3
Beaumanor 2
Lincoln 46½
Loughborough 3½
Nottingham 16 miles *due north*

Woodhouse Eaves lies to the south east.

Take any of the paths down towards Woodhouse Eaves and turn right to **Broombriggs**. This path is sign posted and Broombriggs is worth a visit as a working farm open to the public. It is well waymarked.

(If you wish to go into Woodhouse continue along the road. You can walk through the village street by turning right and rejoin our route by turning right at Pear Tree Inn, Maplewell Road. The path from Broombriggs goes through to

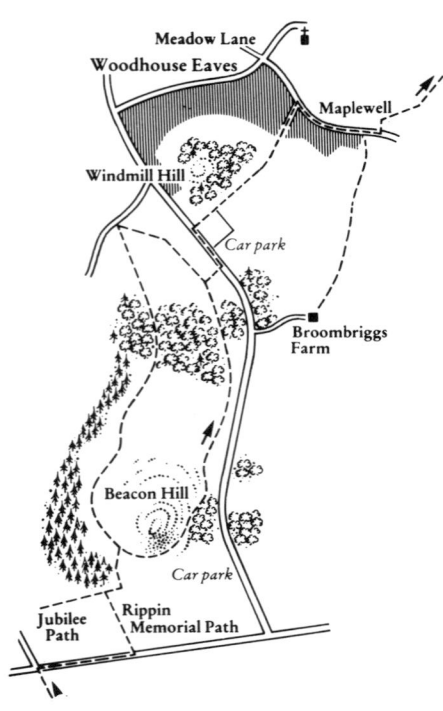

Walk 2 - The Heart of the Forest

Maplewell Road. A second path goes to the left of the car park and continues uphill, slightly left, to a well marked path beside Windmill Hill.

The cinder path beside Windmill Hill becomes Mill Road and leads into Maplewell Road.

Turn right and walk up **Maplewell Road** away from Woodhouse Eaves until the houses end. Turn left just before a big, detached, half-timbered stone house, number 155, and follow the drive which swings right, behind the house, between wooden rails and then beside a hedge on the right.

In the corner of the next field, near **Maplewell farm** on your right, you need to go diagonally left to a stile in the corner of the field. **(Go round the edge of the field to reach this point, following the hedge on your left.)**

From the stile you are going to walk across the golf course and it's a good idea to get your bearings so that you can concentrate on your route and keep an eye open for golf balls and footpath signs.

You are going to turn right and follow the hedge on your right and end up straight ahead, just to the right of **Spring Hill wood**, which will be in front of you - but to get there the golf course directs you with lots of notices along little remains of hedges to your right and sharp left turns and bits of open fairway.

From Spring Hill wood keep close to the hedge on your left until you reach the Cropston Road, by a footpath sign. Immediately opposite, a narrow footpath takes you uphill between a fence and hedge. When you emerge into an open field you will be close to a wall on your right. You need to move over to the hedge on your left and continue up this long, steep and narrow field to the road at the top.

Turn left here along the road to the T junction with **Hunts Hill car park** opposite. Go through the car park and take the main route up to **Old John**. Walk along the ridge and descend to **Newton Linford** past the war memorial and the circular grove of trees called Tyburn. The church spire can be seen just beyond the car park.

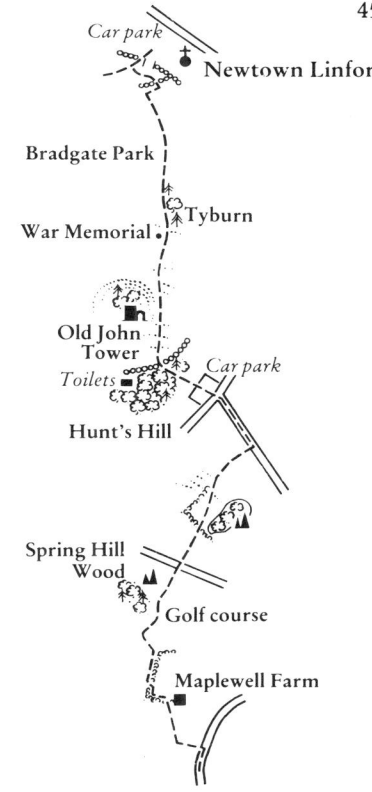

Walk 2 - The Heart of the Forest

CHARNWOOD CIRCUIT from Ulverscroft Priory to Copt Oak
continued from page 42.

Pass *Ulverscroft Priory* on your left and continue close to the wall on your left, which borders the lake. **(Ignore the unfriendly signs which warn you that the area is private and that you can be seen from the house. Your path is a right of way).**

Walk along two fields with the wall, hedge and stream on your left until you reach the footbridge near the corner of the second field. (This footbridge is only a slim plank in a usually muddy area. Cross it as best you can). Continue walking by the stream, now on your right, through a boggy wetland area, managed by the Leicestershire Trust.

Emerge, muddy-booted, in an open field with woodland on your right and walk uphill towards *Poultney Wood*. You need to cross the hedge and stream on your right in the top corner of the field and continue close to the wood on your left. There is a handgate ahead of you (a little to your right) and a good path leads through this straight little stretch of wood.

Walk steeply uphill in the next, open field with the wood on your left, turning round to admire the marvellous views back over the route you have taken.

At the top of the hill the path swings right and follows the remains of an old walled track (now replaced with wooden fencing). Meet the road near *Copt Oak farm* (formerly Whitcroft's farm).

The footpath sign is just a little to your left, on the other side of the road. The path keeps close to the wall on your left crossing it at a point where it juts out. Keep in the same direction, with the wall on your right. At the radio masts, swing right, along the narrow neck of the field which leads into a narrow path behind the church. It bends left to join the road near *Copt Oak* pub, Youth Hostel and Church.

CHARNWOOD CIRCUIT continues on page 58.

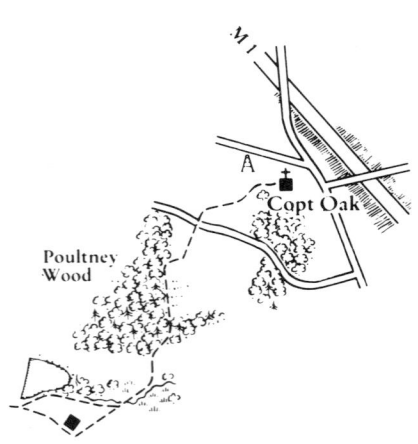

Walk 3 -

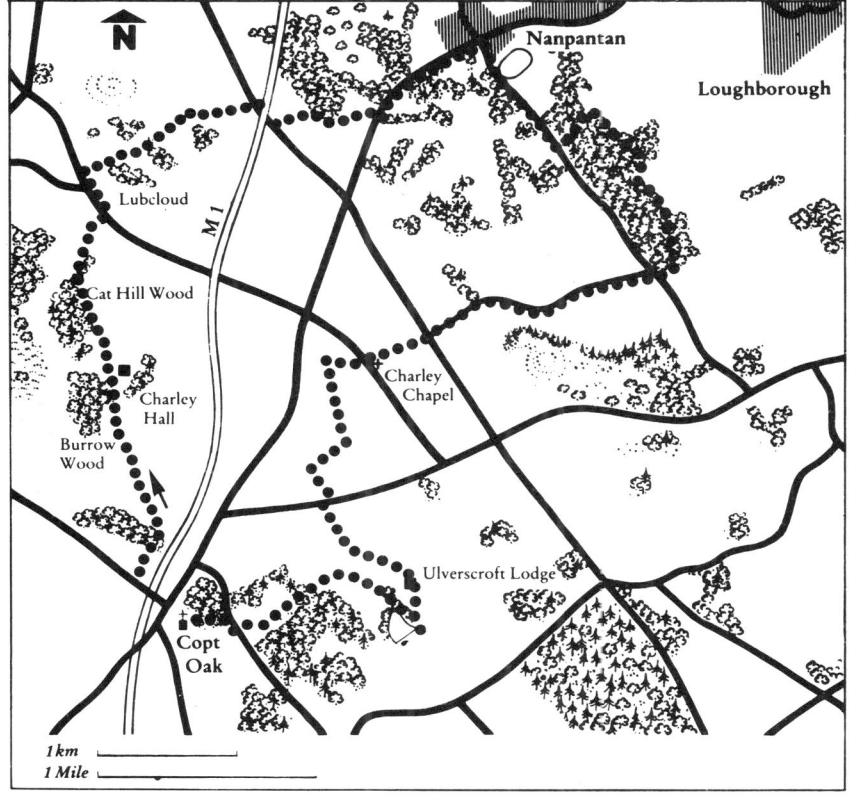

Walk 3 - From Copt Oak Out to the Outwoods

Introduction

From Copt Oak, where swanimote courts were held for disputes and offences committed in Charnwood, we can now set off to see what offences have been committed on the forest in the name of progress and civilization. The walk starts from the Youth Hostel, where cyclists have been heard to complain that Leicestershire is not, as they were led to believe, flat! It immediately crosses the M1 motorway which seems like a 20th century attempt to flatten it, by gouging out its stone to make a runway for fast vehicles. Yet once across the motorway which bi-sects Charnwood we enter the district of Charley and cross over the lands of the original Charley Priory, where Augustinian monks cleared the land for settlement and farming after 1190.

They sited their priory in the beautiful, secluded valley, well-watered by the spring which runs into the Blackbrook. On its site there now stands Charley Hall, which includes some features of the old building. The view we get of the house is not very impressive, as it is hidden by other buildings. But the fields around it are very interestingly full of bumps and hollows and a sunken roadway leads past the hall to Rock farm.

Our way goes past the old Cat Hill wood and through The Mires (where scouts camp) to Lubcloud, near Oaks in Charnwood.

Oaks in Charnwood has a little Enclosure church, opened on 18th June, 1815, the date of the Battle of Waterloo and containing trophies of lances used in that battle. From the field beside the church, there is a spectacular view of Ives Head, the rocky outcrop which was the site of the swanimote court for Shepshed manor. From the top of Lubcloud you can look back over the little hamlet of Oaks in Charnwood to Mt. St. Bernard's Abbey beyond and in the other direction you can see right across the Loughborough plain.

This is where you become aware once more of the 20th century, for you have before you the marvels of civil engineering in the shape of the M1 motorway and, on the crest of the hill beyond it, the vast expanse of Longcliffe quarry. Once past Longcliffe you descend to the fringes of the forest and need to walk two miles along pavementless Enclosure roads to walk via Nanpantan to the Outwoods.

The Outwoods, a gift to the nation since 1946-7 has a Nature Trail and the routes through the woods make a very welcome relief from road walking. Jubilee Wood is a lovely additional gift (1977). Pocket Gate, at the end of the wood, has remains of old sheep dips with sluice gates. This was one of the "ways through" for stock from Loughborough and the farm land to the wild hunting and grazing country beyond the pale.

The Dean's Lane route up to Beacon Hill and Charley Chapel is delightful, passing Blackbird's Nest (now an impressive house) where you have, on your left, dramatic views of the "Devil's profile" of Beacon Hill.

You can make a little detour on to Beacon Hill before returning to the Charley Chapel route, which then goes to Ulverscroft Lodge and through Poultney Wood.

And so, back again to Copt Oak. There are no bus routes through the village. But the pub can be recommended for refreshment to spur you on to a two mile road walk into Markfield. Or you could try the Youth Hostel for a bed for the night.

A marvellous 11 mile excursion through history.

Walk 3 - From Copt Oak Out to the Outwoods

Bardon Hill from Warren Hills

Walk 3 - From Copt Oak Out to the Outwoods

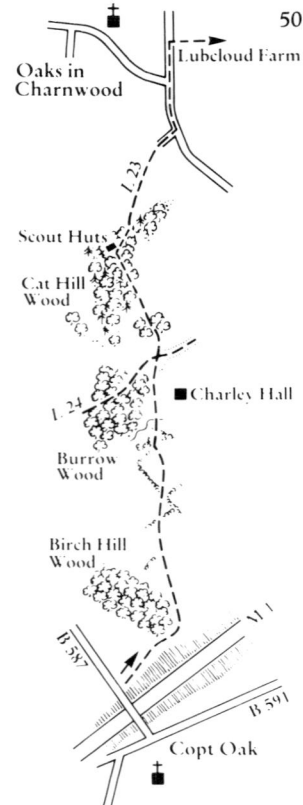

VIA OAKS IN CHARNWOOD, LUBCLOUD, NANPANTAN, POCKET GATE, BEACON HILL, POULTNEY WOOD. (11 MILES)

The pub, the Copt Oak, welcomes walkers and has a big car park. The village also has a telephone box, twin radio masts, visible for miles, and a Youth Hostel.

With the pub on your right, walk to the road junction and turn right along the B591 to Quorn and then left along the B587 to Whitwick. Cross the M1 motorway and turn right along the footpath which goes beside it. After two fields move slightly left to skirt **Birch Hill wood** and go down to the far corner of the field. Cross the farm track on your right and continue in the same direction for three fields. (The first stile is halfway along the hedge, the second is halfway along the hedge on your right (across the corner of the field) and the third is in the bottom right corner of the field, at the edge of the wood.)

Walk parallel with the edge of the wood to the gate opposite and then go diagonally right down to the bottom corner of the field by **Burrow Wood**.

Cross the wall (the gate on the right is usually locked and barbed) and then cross the stream by the big flat stones to the fence opposite.

Walk with the wood on your left until you get level with **Charley Hall** (rather modestly hidden behind a worker's house) and then turn left through the gate and right, to walk with a tree-lined sunken way on your right, going downhill until the remains of an old wall appear on your left. Cross this old wall to reach a stile in the far wall (white painted sign on a stone) about 40 yards up from the corner of the field.

Walk through a small stretch of woodland and emerge with **Cat Hill wood** on your left beyond the wall.

Keep close to the wall and go through two more stiles in the corner of the next two fields and one a little to your right near some scout huts, in a long narrow neck of woodland. The path goes right, passing the scout huts, to a stile on the far side of the wood in the corner of a field.

Walk diagonally right across this field, crossing a track and making for the far corner where an old lane between walls

Walk 3 - From Copt Oak Out to the Outwoods

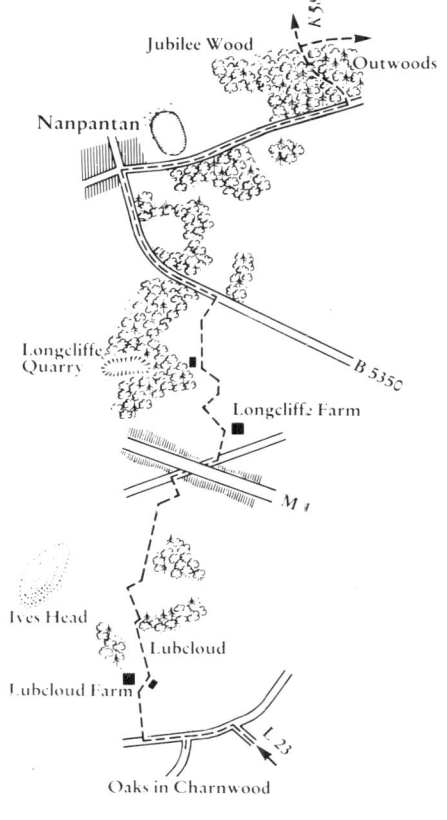

meets a stream. Walk up the lane to the road and turn left towards the cheerful little tower of *Oaks in Charnwood church*.

(The CHARNWOOD CIRCUIT JOINS THE ROUTE HERE, from page 67.

Keep straight on this road towards Shepshed for one field past the Oaks in Charnwood road junction. Turn right, up the path to *Lubcloud farm* and go straight through the farmyard and the middle of the field beyond, to the top of the hill, where you meet the corner of a small wood.

Here you are on top of the Cloud, a fine place to stop to admire the views over Oaks in Charnwood to Mount St. Bernard's Abbey. On the other side of the hill you will overlook the whole plain of Loughborough with the motorway cutting through.

A little woodland track takes you round the wood's corner. After about 20 yards, leave it by the first gate on the left, to walk downhill, close to the

Walk 3 - From Copt Oak Out to the Outwoods

hedge on your left. A little to your right, in the hedge ahead of you, a gate leads into the next field, where you have the hedge on your left again. **Look ahead at this point, for you are soon going to cross the motorway and go up by the farm on the far side of it, to the plantation at the top of the hill.**

To get there, aim for the bottom corner of the field, in line with the farm and turn left when you meet a concrete track, which leads up to the road. Turn right when you meet the road and go under the motorway to the farm drive.

Turn left to go to *Longcliffe farm*. When you reach the old stable buildings, take the gate on your left and go up the middle of the field to the plantation at the top.

Longcliffe Quarry has, regrettably, just extended its activities here and diverted the path around the wood, so you need to turn right and walk with the hedge on your left for two fields until you come to a thinning in the trees, just past the house in the trees on your left. Make your way through the gap and pass the house and stables on your left. Join the farm drive down to the road and turn left along the B5350 to *Nanpantan*.

There is, unfortunately, no way to avoid the one mile of road walking unless some public benefactor should dedicate a right of way across Nanpantan Hall land or Longcliffe Quarry land. The Charnwood roads are very dangerous for road walkers.

Pass Nanpantan Hall lodge and the little church of St. Mary in Charnwood and turn right at the cross roads, near Priory pub, *Nanpantan*.

Another stretch of pavementless road takes you past the reservoir and uphill to Jubilee Wood on your left.

You can walk through the wood, keeping parallel with the road, moving to your left when you meet the K58 path which separates *Jubilee Wood* from *the Outwoods*. This is the path which leads to Loughborough and will take you round the edge of the Outwoods.

Stay in the wood and follow the path as it turns right and keep following the edge of the wood all the way to *Pocket Gate*. It is lovely to walk in the wood and to have fine open views to your left. You pass through only two patches of wood where your view is restricted. In the second you may see a house on your left and at this point the path begins to swing right to bring you out on the road again.

Turn left for 100 yards to a cross-roads (Pocket Gate and Dean's Lane).

Turn right up *Dean's Lane*, a quiet road this time, passing Blackbird's Nest and noting the fascinating "devil's profile" rock of *Beacon Hill* on the left.

At the top of the hill pass the fine old round towered farm of Beacon Cottage and come to a belt of trees on your left, signposted to Beacon Hill.

(This is Jubilee footpath. Beacon Hill is only a field away and makes a good picnic stop.)

CHARNWOOD CIRCUIT walkers continue over Beacon Hill and take any of the paths which lead downhill to Woodhouse Eaves. See page 34.

Walk 3

Continue down Dean's Lane to the T junction. Cross the B5330 road and go over the stile beside the gate opposite and walk down the field with the hedge on your right. Cross the stream and walk uphill. At the top of the field the path goes right and then left to continue in the same direction, with the hedge on the left, up to ***Charley Chapel***. Cross the road slightly to your right and walk, moving slightly right, to ***Cattens Rough***, a walled plantation. Cross the far wall to the right of the plantation. (There is a gate in the corner of the field, which you can go through, although, strictly speaking the correct crossing is downhill to your right where there is a stile.) Turn left and keep this wall on your left for three fields. Pass a little old quarry tip.

Follow the farm track as it swings right, up to the corner of the field and then left, between walls. (***Bawdon Castle***).

On your right you can now see the twin masts of Copt Oak. Turn towards

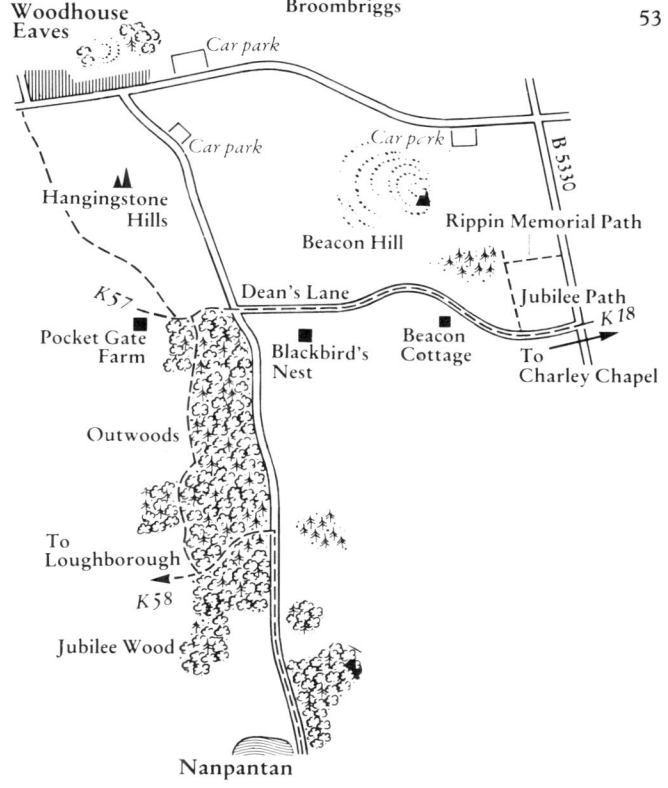

Walk 3 - From Copt Oak Out to the Outwoods

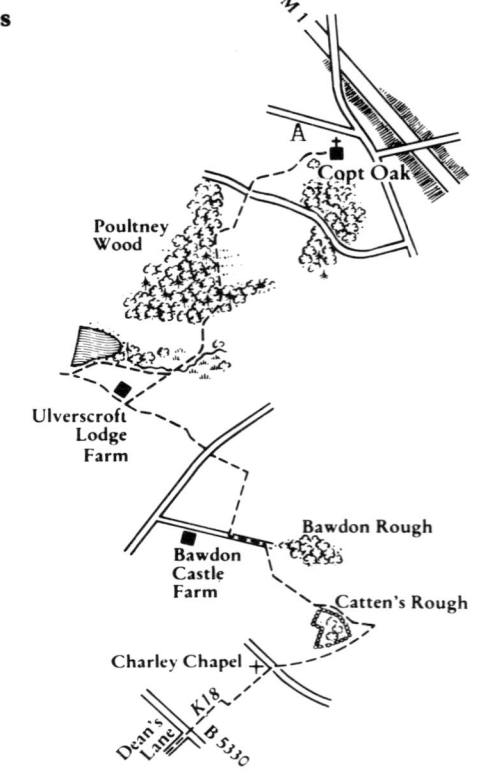

them at the first gate and walk downhill with the hedge on the left for two fields. Turn left at the stile in the corner and then right to go through the gate and turn left again to walk with the hedge on your left. At the road cross to the footpath opposite. This is signposted and waymarked. Walk with the hedge on your left for three fields to *Ulverscroft Lodge*.

Just before the cattle pens, the footpath turns back on itself. You need to turn sharp right and go through a small new plantation and continue in the same direction to reach the far corner of this same field, (where you join the FP from Ulverscroft Priory to Copt Oak). Here there is a sign and a stile leading into a wooded marshy area, near Poultney Wood. You have to cross a stream to get to the stile and then go through a small patch of wetland, following the stream on your right.

This area is managed by the Leicester & Rutland Trust for Nature Conservation so you get your boots wet in a good cause!

Emerge in an open field with the hedge on your right. Go to the gate in

Walk 3 - From Copt Oak Out to the Outwoods

the top corner and cross the stream. Then follow the hedge on your left to the bridle gate into **Poultney Wood**. A small stretch of woodland leads you to an open field. Go uphill towards the radio masts for two fields, moving right in the second to a gateway in the wall ahead. Follow the track with the remains of an old wall on your left and turn left at the road. The footpath sign takes you into the field on the opposite side of the road, (Whitcroft's Lane). Walk with the hedge on your left, directly towards the radio mast. Cross the fence to walk with the same hedge on your right and turn sharp right when you reach the mast. Walk with the hedge on your right along a narrow field to a path which leads round the church to the road, near the telephone box and the pub, **The Copt Oak**.

Walk 4 - From Copt Oak West

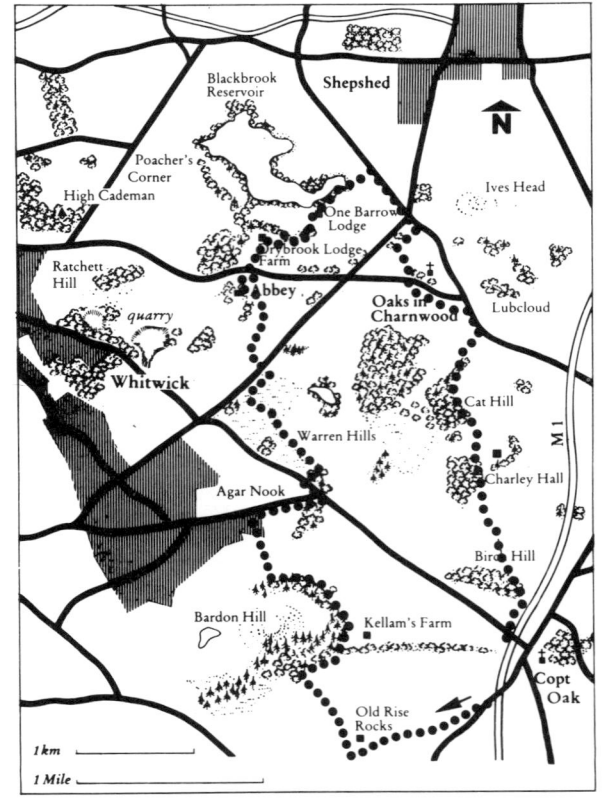

This walk begins from Copt Oak and crosses the M1 motorway (but by a different route from Walk 3. It returns to Copt Oak via the route described in that walk but from the opposite direction).

It is a walk which could be quite adventurous if you chose to follow a pre-1971 map or guide book, for your first landmark is Bardon Hill, the highest point in Leicestershire. It is well worth a trip up to the summit, for the view and for the spectacle of the vast quarrying operations, but you must return by the same route to the path below and walk right round the foot of the hill to continue. From the lovely path along the Warren Hills you can look back to Bardon and see the dramatically scarred hill, with its sad and scrawny dark conifers clinging to what is left of the once green hill, which was Whitwick's deer park.

A good mid-way stopping point on this walk is Mt. St. Bernard's Abbey. It is a modern construction, built in 1835, the first Catholic abbey in England since the Reformation. It is a restrained and elegant building, visible for miles. The monks work in the fields and in the pottery and in the small shop which sells books, cards, pottery and farm produce. Visitors are welcome and there are toilets provided, too.

You can shorten the walk at this point, by walking along the road to Oaks in Charnwood or you can risk another adventure by going across Blackbrook Reservoir, which necessitates a 200 pace stretch of walking along a lane which has, since 1954, been declared a private carriageway. (But no-one actually insists that you have written permission to walk the short

Walk 4 - From Copt Oak West Towards Whitwick

distance involved and the footpaths on each side of the lane are so obviously legal rights of way that no-one is likely to turn you back from the lane. I bring it to your attention, however, because it is the only bit of the route described in this book that is not absolutely established as a public right of way). A small diversion is at present being negotiated and should be clearly signposted.

Blackbrook is a beautiful little reservoir in a setting of pinkish volcanic rocks. You can loiter on the bridge and watch the water birds which feed there.

The little walk over the hill to Oaks in Charnwood is delightful with marvellous views of Ives Head. There are no real amenities in the village, which is merely a hamlet, with a small Enclosure Award church, opened in 1815 (at the time of the Battle of Waterloo). The last stretch of the walk may seem familiar, if you have already done walk 3. It goes through the Blackbrook valley, along its wooded slopes to Charley Hall. From this quiet, secluded spot we return to Copt Oak beyond the motorway.

This walk can be started from Agar Nook, as described in the post-script to the Instructions for Walking.

A good 8½ miles if you include Blackbrook.
About 7½ miles if you choose the road route to Oaks in Charnwood.
No bus escape routes, unless you walk into Whitwick from Agar Nook (1½ miles) or from Mt. St. Bernard's (1½ miles).

DIRECTIONS TO TOURISTS

It must always be borne in mind that there is **no common-land** in the forest, and therefore the visitor is always on sufferance. Never fail, therefore, when desirous of seeing plantations or enclosed grounds, to procure the occupier's permission to ramble about them. A note, addressed to the owner of the estate, a few days previously, may save a pleasant party from a summary dismissal by the keeper.

Bradgate is always open to the public on Mondays.

Having obtained the permission, which is generally most courteously granted, shew, by carefully closing gates, avoiding disturbance of the game, damage to the fences, & c., that you desire to reciprocate the courtesy.

None of the mansions of the forest are at all of a public character, and can therefore only be viewed by special permission.

Good rustic accomodation can be had at Groby or Newtown Lindford for visitors to Bradgate, & c.

There is no publichouse at Woodhouse, but Woodhouse Eaves will afford stabling and refreshment for visitors to Pocket Gate, Beacon, & c. None of the villages afford style, but in all of them stabling, & c., and comfortable accomodation are to be found.

1858. Companion to Charnwood Forest.

Walk 4 - From Copt Oak West Towards Whitwick

VIA BARDON HILL, AGAR NOOK,
MOUNT ST. BERNARD'S ABBEY,
BLACKBROOK RESERVOIR, OAKS IN
CHARNWOOD. (8½ MILES)

From Copt Oak pub, pass the church and youth hostel and turn left along the B591 towards Stanton-under-Bardon. Cross the bridge over the M1 motorway. Go diagonally right, down the embankment, to a wicket gate and continue in the same direction, to cut across the corner of the first field to a farm gate. Keep in the same direction across the next field and cross a double fence beside a tree.

Walk with the hedge on your right for two fields, crossing the track to *Old Rise Rocks farm*. Keep the hedge and the track on your right and pass the outcrop of Rise Rocks on your left.

Pass the farm and cross the stile in the corner of the field. Turn right and pass the end of the farm track. Continue downhill parallel with the hedge on your right. Cross a stream and the hedge beyond it. Go up to the left corner of the small wood ahead.

(The stile on the right is from the path from Kellams farm) Continue with the wood on your right until a stile brings

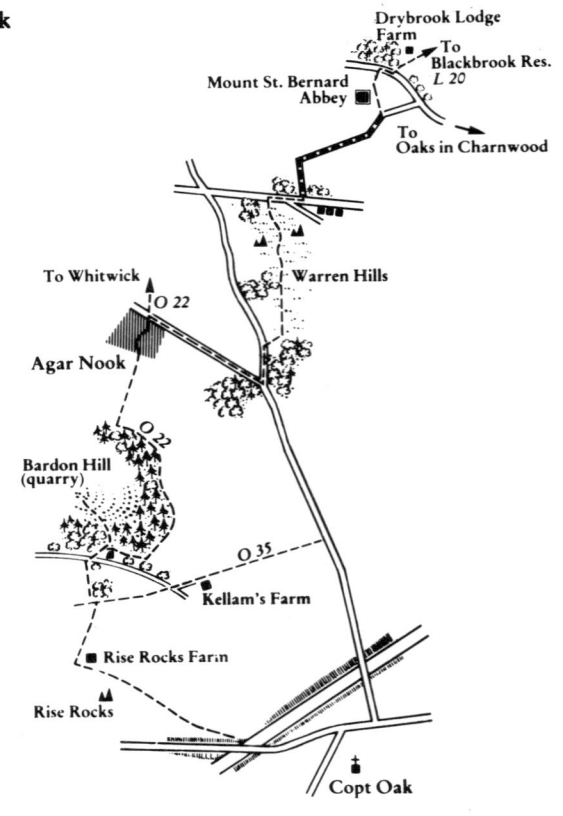

Walk 4 - From Copt Oak West Towards Whitwick

you out on the drive from Bardon Hall to Copt Oak. Turn right for a few yards and then make your way across a piece of rough, boggy ground to the farm on your left.

Pass between the farmhouse and its outbuildings and climb the bank to a gap in the wall beyond the farm, to the foot of *Bardon Hill*.

From here there is a narrow path up through the trees to the summit of Bardon Hill and it is worth climbing to the top to see the fantastic views and the extent of the quarry. The hill is still the highest in Leicestershire but it is now only a hollow shell, constantly eroded by quarrying. Our path once went straight over the hill to Agar Nook and Whitwick. We now have to return to the foot of the hill and make a big semi-circular sweep around it.

Follow the wall behind the farmhouse. At the cross road of tracks, fork right and walk downhill to the edge of the wood and then swing left to follow the bottom edge of the wood for a mile right round to the other side of the quarry. When you come to the quarry bank, ahead of you, turn right. A well-trodden footpath leads through to the housing estate of *Agar Nook* and continues in the same direction to meet the Coalville-Copt Oak road.

From Agar Nook to Mt. St. Bernard's abbey, via the Warren Hills.

Turn right, up the Coalville-Copt Oak road to the T-junction. (The Bull's Head pub is 50 yards to the right) Our route goes left along the road towards Whitwick for 100 yards. When you have passed the house on your left, cross the road and enter the *Warren Hills* nature reserve by the gate at the footpath sign.

Cross over the field to a gateway at the corner of the wood opposite and continue along the same track for a short distance, until on your left you come to the corner of a wall projecting into the field.

Pass through the gap and keep the stone wall on your right as you walk the length of the hills, with rocky outcrops on your left. Continue in the same direction until you reach the Coalville-Shepshed road at the footpath sign.

Turn right and walk along the road for 300 yards until you reach the lodge gates to *Mount St. Bernard's Abbey*. Turn left and follow the drive, which soon swings right and leads to the abbey.

Walk 4 - From Copt Oak West Towards Whitwick

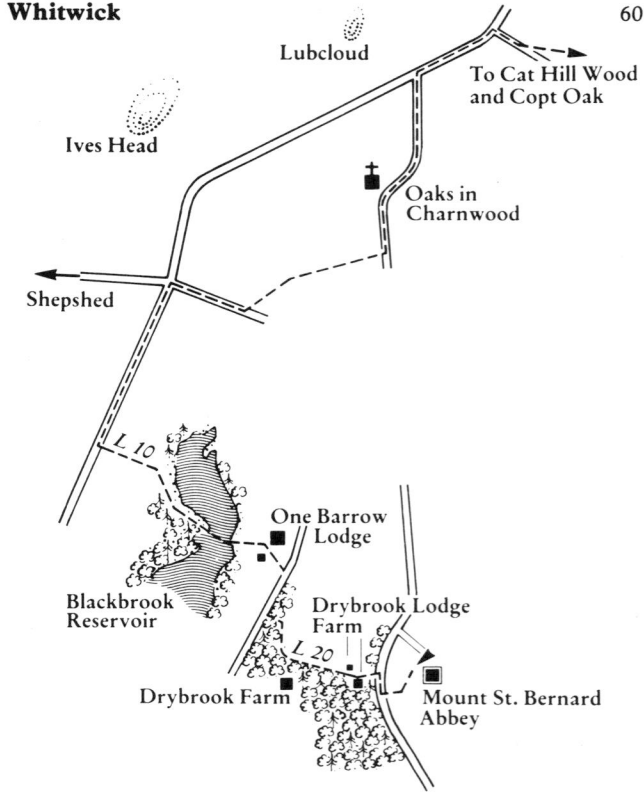

If you follow the drive from the abbey out onto the road you can turn right and walk along the road all the way to Oaks in Charnwood if you do not wish to take the Blackbrook reservoir route.

If you wish to continue on the Blackbrook reservoir route, continue along the drive from the Abbey car park until it bends right. Then cross the fence by the gate straight ahead of you (ignoring the gate on your left which leads to the Guests' quarters).

Keep close to the Abbey grounds on your left. A stile at the end of the field leads you right down to the road through a narrow little wooded track. Turn right, along the road, to ***Drybrook Lodge farm***.

From Mt. St. Bernard's Abbey to Oaks in Charnwood via Blackbrook.

At ***Drybrook Lodge farm*** turn down the track passing the farm on your left and farmbuildings on the right. **(You might be asked if you "need assistance" at this point as the lane at the end of this path is a disputed right of way, but as this**

Walk 4 - From Copt Oak West Towards Whitwick

path and the one on the other side of the lane are rights of way you cannot be turned back here and no attempt is usually made to prevent you using the small stretch of disputed way to the next farm).

Walk along the L20 path with the hedge and wood on your left. At the far end of the field turn right (ignoring the farm track straight ahead). The footpath goes from the corner of the field. (It is sometimes obstructed). Cross into the newly planted wooded area and swing left to meet the lane. Turn right at the lane for 200 yards. Turn left to pass *One Barrow Lodge farm*, moving left to join a lane which leads to Blackbrook reservoir. Continue to the road, by the footpath sign at *Botany Bay*.

(CHARNWOOD CIRCUIT continues on page 67.)

Turn right for half a mile along the road to the cross roads and then turn right, uphill. Turn left at the second hedge on the left and walk with it on your right, to the corner of the field. Cross the double stile junction with three other fields and emerge in the one facing the road with the church on your left and a sports pavilion opposite. Go downhill to the gate by the pavilion and turn left along the road to *Oaks in Charnwood*.

Pass the church on your left and walk to the T junction. At the T junction turn right. Pass one field and then turn right again down an old walled track. When the wall ends, go diagonally left to the corner of the long field towards the wood by Loughborough Scouts Centre. The path goes through a narrow neck of woods past scout huts to emerge with *Cat Hill wood* on the right. Walk with Cat Hill wood on your right for three fields. At the end of the wood wall a little woodland path leads you into the bottom corner of a field with a spinney at the far side.

If you started at Agar Nook or Whitwick and wish to take a short cut back to Kellam's farm and Agar Nook or Whitwick, omitting Copt Oak you can turn right at this point and go up to the corner of Burrow Wood to join the O35 path which passes Charley Mill

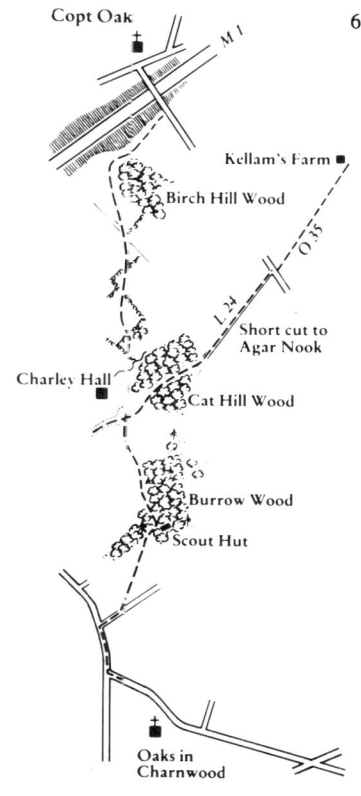

Walk 4 - From Copt Oak West Towards Whitwick

farm and Kellam's farm and swings round Bardon Hill. (See the postscript to this walk).

To reach Copt Oak go towards the spinney and move up to the far right corner where it meets the corner of **Burrow Wood**. Go through the gate and walk with Burrow Wood on your right passing **Charley Hall** on your left.

Cross the stream in the bottom corner over big flat stepping stones and cross the wall on the other side, to emerge in the corner of a field. Go uphill, crossing the field diagonally, passing a spinney in the top left corner. Cross to the gate opposite and continue diagonally across the next three fields, crossing a lane to Charley Mill farm and continuing in the same direction to pass the end of **Birch Hill wood** and reach the motorway boundary fence.

Walk with the fence on your left for two fields and turn left to join the road. Cross over the motorway. Turn right and then left to reach the pub, church and youth hostel at **Copt Oak**.

If you wish to take the shorter version of this walk, starting from Agar Nook and omitting Copt Oak:-

Start the walk, as described in Walk 4, from page 59 to page 61 and then insert the following stretch of path from Charley Hall:-

After passing Cat Hill wood, walk to the far side of the field, where you meet the remains of an old wall (only visible as a roughly raised line of ground) just before the raised bank of a sunken tree-lined track and stream bed. Turn right and follow the old wall line uphill to a little corner of Burrow Wood.

Go through the wood and go left on a farm lane from Charnwood Lodge which passed the drive to Charley Mill farm. Cross over the main Whitwick-Copt Oak road and walk with the hedge on your right along the O35 track to **Kellam's farm**.

Just past the farm house you meet the long tree-lined mile-long drive leading from the old Bardon Hall into Copt Oak. The path to Bardon Hill goes off to the right from a little way along to the right on this drive. But to join the route described in Walk 4 from Old Rise Rocks, you should cross the drive and continue in the same direction, walking with hedge on your right, to pass the little rectangular fox covert, then turn right to reach the foot of **Bardon Hill**. (as on page 59).

Walk 5 -

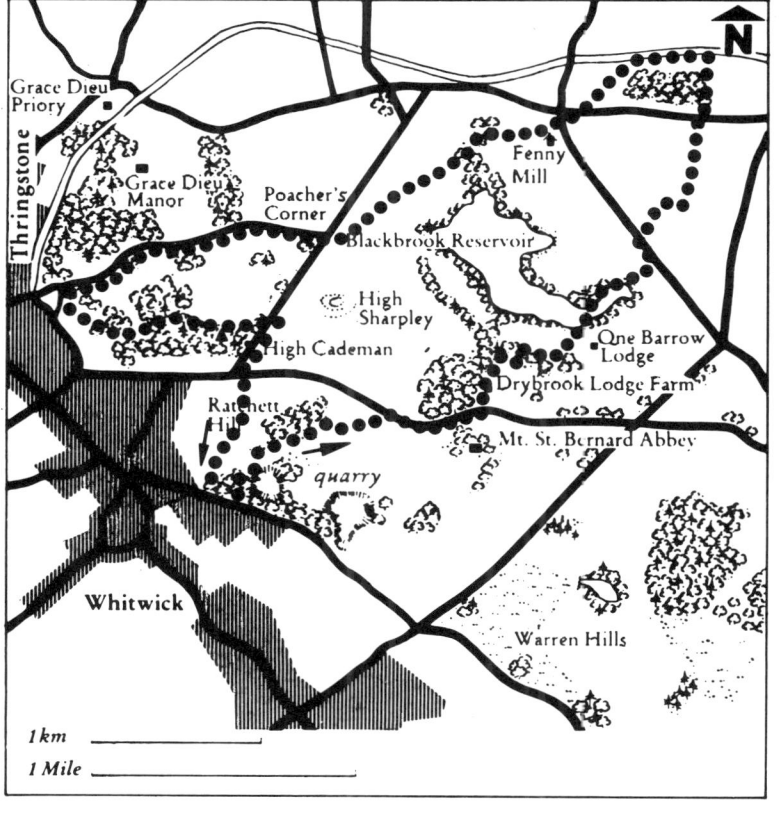

Walk 5 - From Whitwick in Search of an Extinct Volcano

Introduction

Walk 5 might well be sub-titled 'Diversions and Closures' as it passes over the Garendon Estates where much 'rationalization' of footpaths has taken place.

I should like to dedicate it to Mr. Ernest Colledge of Whitwick, who loves these paths and who has done so much over the years to preserve and protect them.

This walk goes via Mount St. Bernard's and circles the volcanic area of High Sharpley. It starts, rather unpromisingly perhaps, in Whitwick town street, but soon becomes glorious as it rises beyond Spring Hill quarry, where the whole panorama opens up with views over High Sharpley and Gun Hill and the distinctive peak of Ives Head, where Shepshed's swanimote court was held.

To see the site of the volcano which erupted more than 570 million years ago turn right after you have passed Ratchett Hill and before you reach Mt St Bernard's abbey. The track round the quarry affords spectacular views down to the quarry pool, where the original core of the volcano is now being quarried.

The main section of the walk has proved somewhat difficult to describe, because it passes over the Garendon Estates, which has had a long history of disputes over rights of way and which at the moment is undertaking a massive 'rationalization' of footpaths. This has meant a description of the present existing routes and the proposed diversions, which might become law before this book appears. **The diversions are contained in bold print**.

There is one section of the route which is not at present a right of way, a 200 yard length of lane which was declared private at an appeals tribunal in 1954 after it was put on the Definitive Map in 1952. You can write for permission to walk along this stretch, but you are not likely to be turned back, and certainly cannot be turned back while you are still on the legitimate footpaths at each end of the short disputed stretch. We hope that we can find some way of joining the two footpaths soon, as the present position is clearly most unsatisfactory. An alternative route along the "Black Ash" path has been proposed.

The short stretch of dismantled railway near Shepshed is interesting because it is the Charnwood Forest railway, which follows the bed of the disused Charnwood Forest canal, from Loughborough via Grace Dieu and Thringstone and Whitwick. The canal had been built in 1791 as a link between railways which loaded wagons on a specially constructed float at Thringstone to take them to the Loughborough railway at Nanpantan. But in 1799 the canal burst its banks, the water was lost and the canal never repaired. So ended a complex system of rail and canal link for transporting coal to Leicester.

The line makes a pleasant walk on the outskirts of Shepshed, enabling one to by-pass the busy A512 road. It has recently been dedicated as a 'Jubilee' public footpath. The first part is gravelled and has not yet acquired the rubbish which the other end of the railway, (near Grace Dieu, Thringstone) shamefully has. Our walk, however, does not continue so far along the railway but goes, via "Paradise", to the end of the Blackbrook reservoir, where again we have impressive views of volcanic High Sharpley, this time from the north. High Sharpley is not actually a public right of way so I have not described the route across the summit. But Whitwick commoners continue a long tradition of asserting their rights of access, while

From High Sharpley

Walk 5 - From Whitwick in Search of an Extinct Volcano

acknowledging the landlord's ownership of the soil, the trees and the game! They all seem able to describe vividly the magnificent views from the top of High Sharpley right over Blackbrook reservoir and all round the plain beyond Charnwood forest. Many talk of knowing the family who used to live in the stark Gun Hill House, built into the rock. The rocks are also used by climbers.

From the top one can also see the line of the path which must have come from Fenney Hill (near the present windmill) via the Hermitage and so into Whitwick before the Blackbrook reservoir was built. The first Blackbrook reservoir was constructed in the 18th century but, like the Charnwood forest canal which it was meant to feed, was very short lived. It broke its dam in 1799 due to earthquake damage! and was dismantled in 1804. The present reservoir replaced it in 1906.

From Poacher's Corner you have a choice of taking the short route, along the Swanimote Road, passing close to the Swanimote Rock and High Sharpley with its pinnacles of rock and High Cademan: or the longer route which goes along the quieter and prettier minor road into Thringstone. Along this lane there are lovely views of the Swanimote rock and High Sharpley and Gun Hill beyond it and you pass close to the site of the old Swanimote Oak in the field beside Swannymote farm. (The present oak tree was reputedly taken from an acorn from the original!).

Further along the lane you have a good view over the Grace Dieu Manor, now a school. In the valley beyond it, and out of sight, the remains of Grace Dieu Priory stand.

Our route, however turns left at Thringstone to go through Cademan Wood. In the wood stands High Cademan Rock, which is worth the very small detour from our path, through the wood. There are many little paths and small crags in the woods. It is a favourite haunt of Whitwick folk and the views from the top of High Cademan are spectacular.

All told, it's an exhilarating 6 or 8 miles in volcano country. The most beautiful part of the forest (No shelter from the rain, however, and no shops en route, unless you call in at the abbey at Mount St. Bernards).

Walk 5 - From Whitwick in Search of an Extinct Volcano

VIA MOUNT ST. BERNARD'S ABBEY, BLACKBROOK RESERVOIR, WHITE HORSE WOOD, WITH AN OPTIONAL EXTRA TO THRINGSTONE. (6 OR 8 MILES)

From Whitwick, go uphill along the Leicester Road until you come to No. 107. **(Ignore the footpath sign beside No. 77 - this is your return route.)**

Follow the track that goes opposite No. 120 and past the quarry bank. Pass a small playing field on your left and keep on the track, which swings right near Tower House. *Ratchett Hill* wood is on your left and a newly seeded quarry slope on your right. Turn right for 100 yards along a track which leads up to the quarry. Turn left at the stile and walk towards *Mt. St. Bernard's Abbey*.

The footpath continues in the direction of Mt. St. Bernard's Abbey, going diagonally over four fields and crossing one farm track, to meet the road at the footpath sign. Turn right and continue along the road towards the abbey. **(A footpath on your right goes up to the abbey through a belt of trees. If you wish to visit it, turn left at the top of the path and walk with Abbey grounds on your right. Turn right at the gate and walk along the drive to the Abbey.)** The road leads to *Oaks in Charnwood*, (1 mile).

(CHARNWOOD CIRCUIT walkers continue past Oaks in Charnwood church, turn left along the Shepshed road and go right, to Lubcloud. See page 51).

To reach Blackbrook reservoir you need to turn left down the drive to *Drybrook Lodge farm*, 100 yards past the footpath turn to Mt. St. Bernard's. Pass the house on your left and take the right hand fork, to continue downhill close to the wood on your left. At the bottom of the field you should turn right to follow the bottom hedge along to the corner of the field. There should be a stile in the corner, but it has been obstructed for a long time and you need to follow a faintly marked track between the newly planted trees to reach the lane.

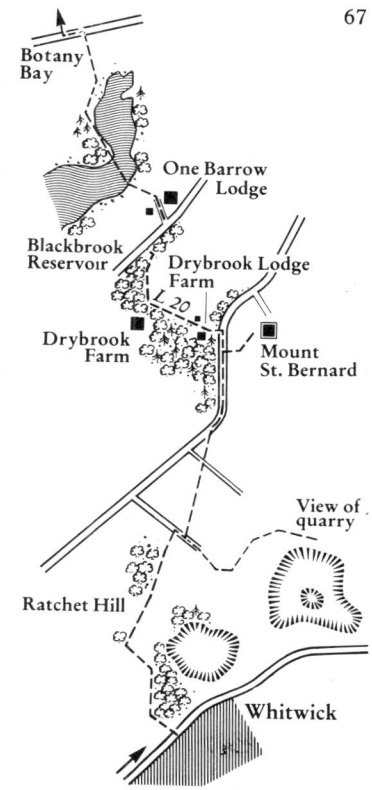

Walk 5 - From Whitwick in Search of an Extinct Volcano

You need to turn right and walk for 200 yards along the lane (a disputed path) to **One Barrow Lodge** and then turn left, passing the farm buildings and a hedge on your right. You are now once again on an acknowledged right of way. Continue on the lane over Blackbrook reservoir and join the road at Botany Bay.

A proposed diversion from Mount St. Bernard's Abbey to Blackbrook reservoir is now being considered. It will, if confirmed, avoid the present disputed area by starting opposite the main lodge gates of the abbey, continuing along the road towards Oaks in Charnwood for 100 yards, passing a spinney on your left and turning left to follow the edge of the spinney (on the old Black Ash path) until you emerge on the One Barrow Lane. You will then simply cross the lane and join the driveway which leads to One Barrow Lodge, swinging left to join the track which goes to the left of the farm.

(THE CHARNWOOD CIRCUIT

JOINS THE WALK HERE from page 61.

From Botany Bay turn left, along the road for one field and then turn right, *towards Shepshed*, at the footpath sign and walk with the hedge on your right. Continue in the same direction in the next (small) field. A stile in the corner, near the house, leads to a lane which takes you between some houses to meet **Brick Kiln Lane** at the T junction. Turn left and walk straight down to the main A512 road (Ashby to Loughborough).

Cross the road and turn right for a short distance to the footpath sign. Turn left along the footpath to **White Horse Wood**.

The path continues due north, passing just inside **White Horse Wood**. It crosses one small stretch of open ground to meet the dismantled railway, recently dedicated as a footpath.

Turn left along the railway path until you reach the railway bridge, where you see White Horse Wood on your left. The L13 path goes to the right of White Horse Wood at this point.

The diversion of the L13 path, if it is accepted, will keep you on the railway line for the length of one more field (200 yards). You will then turn left and walk with the brook on your left, following the hedge on your left until you meet a little track which takes you up the bank of the road.

The L13 path at present leaves the railway line just before the railway bridge and descends into the corner of a big field to the right of White Horse wood. You need to move diagonally uphill, away from the wood on your left, over the brow of the hill and down to the corner of the field. Continue in the same direction across 'Paradise field' and join the little track which goes up the steep bank to the road.

Cross over Tickow Lane cross-roads towards **Fenney Mill** and join Charley Road for a short distance. Here, on your right, is a little lane. By a small Water Board building, cross the fence and cut across the corner of the field to rejoin the lane (which takes a right angle bend) at the stone, squeeze-through stile.

Walk 5

Turn left and follow the lane towards the lovely, landscaped grounds of **Blackbrook reservoir** water works.

Your footpath goes to the right of the main drive, up between walls along a grassy track. Keep the water board wall on your left and go up to the handgate into an undulating open field.

The established route goes diagonally left from the handgate to the fence near a telegraph pole and then to a stile in the hedge on your left and then across the small corner of the next field, to reach 'quarter mile field' which you cross diagonally to reach **Poachers' Corner,** on the Swanimote Road.

(To follow the diversion route, from the handgate turn left and follow the reservoir wood to the corner of the field, cross the (non-existent) stile and turn right to walk with the hedge on your right. At the end of the field do not go straight on to the road, but turn left and walk with the hedge on your right to meet the lane from the Hermitage to Poacher's Corner. Turn right to Poacher's

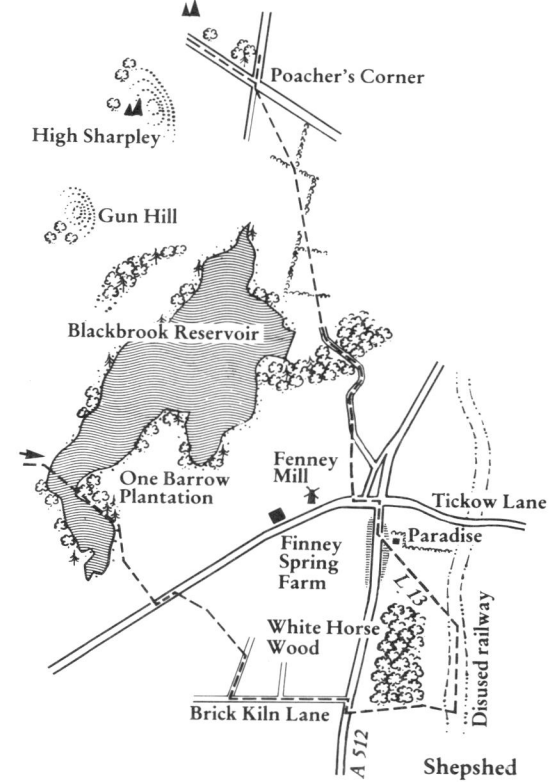

Walk 5

Corner).

From Poacher's Corner you can take a short cut to Whitwick (1 mile) by turning left and walking along Swanimote Road, as in the final paragraph, to Oaks Road. page 71.

From Poacher's Corner to Whitwick, via Thringstone (3 miles):- Go straight down the road opposite (Warren Lane) and walk along it for a mile to Thringstone. Turn left at the road fork, along Carr Lane, past Turry Log cottage. Turn left at the footpath sign (100 yards) and go over the fence-stile to Croson's farm. Cross the fence-stile at the right of the farm and skirt the buildings to reach the fence-stile in the left corner. Continue straight up the next field towards the wood ahead of you.

Cross the fence-stile into the neck of the wood and continue in the same direction across the rough open field of *Cademan Moor*, avoiding the path which goes off to the right. Go through *Cademan Wood*, still continuing in the same direction (due East) passing *High Cademan Rock* on your right. The main track brings you out close to a wall on your left near Swanimote Road, at a gap in the

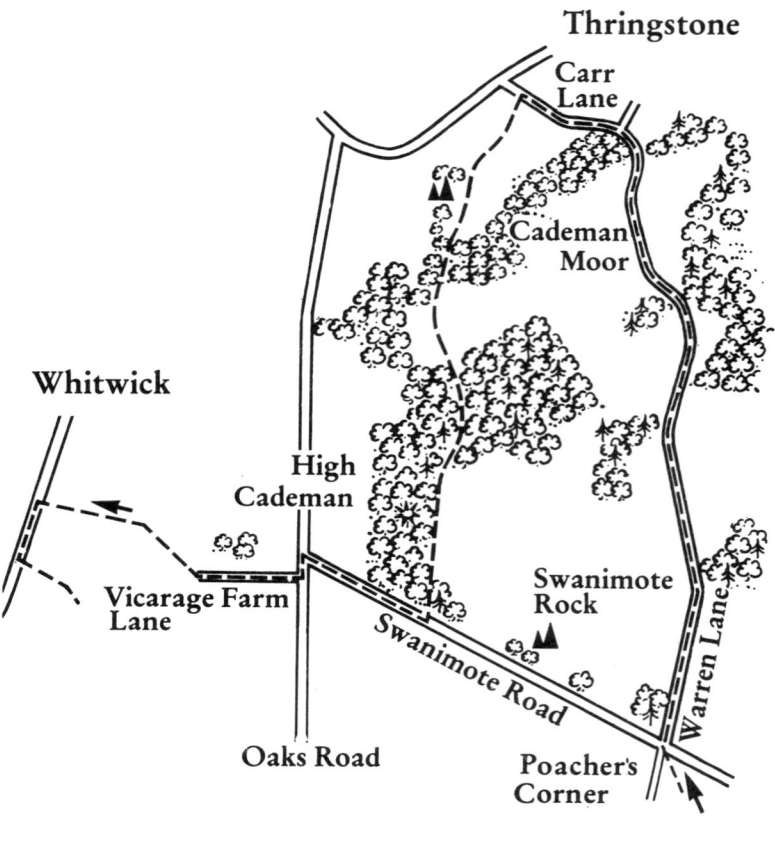

Walk 5 - From Whitwick in Search of an Extinct Volcano

wall, near the footpath sign.
Turn right and walk along the road to the junction with **Oaks Road**. Turn left and then right to walk along Vicarage Farm Lane for 200 yards. Just before the farm, cross the fence-stile on your right (at the F.P. sign), go to the right of the farmhouse, where the wall makes an angle and follow the wall and hedge all the way down into Whitwick, crossing Hogarth Road and emering on Leicester Road at No. 77.
Turn right to the centre of Whitwick.

**(CHARNWOOD CIRCUIT
continues on page 67).
beginning of walk 5.**

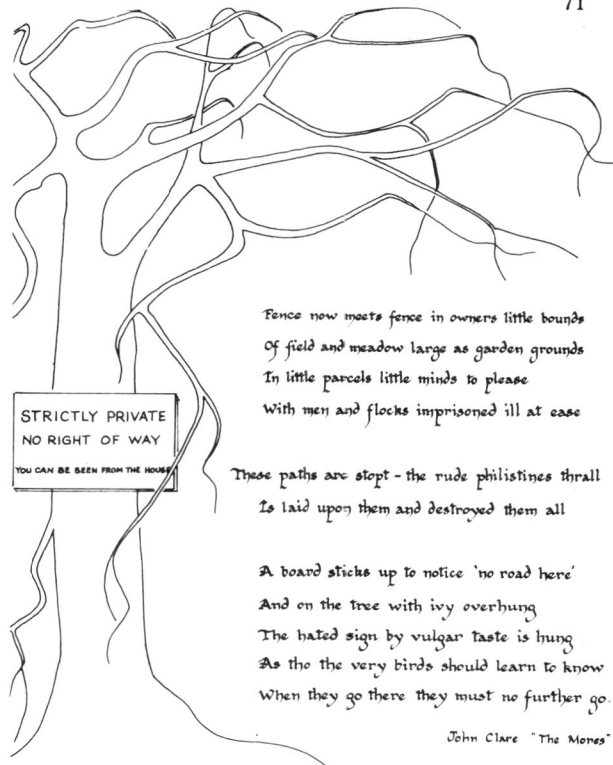

STRICTLY PRIVATE
NO RIGHT OF WAY
YOU CAN BE SEEN FROM THE HOUSE

Fence now meets fence in owners little bounds
Of field and meadow large as garden grounds
In little parcels little minds to please
With men and flocks imprisoned ill at ease

These paths are stopt - the rude philistines thrall
Is laid upon them and destroyed them all

A board sticks up to notice 'no road here'
And on the tree with ivy overhung
The hated sign by vulgar taste is hung
As tho the very birds should learn to know
When they go there they must no further go.

John Clare "The Mores"

"Ah! the old woman was right that bade us take this road".

W. Napier Reeve (Eliot Roscoe)
Bradgate Park 1849

Pinfold, Anstey

Ways In to Charnwood

As the title suggests, the following short walks are intended as ways in to the walks already described, and to the Charnwood circuit. Return routes are also described. By themselves, using just short stretches of other walks they make very pleasant little circuits. A map indicates, better than words, how the combinations can be made. See page 4.

Way In: From Leicester and Back

Introduction

It is very satisfying to walk straight from the busy city right into the countryside, and this walk makes a lovely, long Sunday afternoon walk "just to the park and back." (4 miles out and 4 miles back!)

It is specially designed for city dwellers who cannot afford the bus fare and for those who want to remind themselves of the feeling of travelling in the days before the ubiquitous motor car took over from legs and feet.

There are fine views of Old John, getting closer all the time once you reach Glenfrith Way.

Country Code

WHEREVER YOU GO, FOLLOW THE COUNTRY CODE

Enjoy the countryside and respect its life and work
Guard against all risk of fire
Fasten all gates
Keep your dogs under close control
Keep to public paths across farmland
Use gates and stiles to cross fences, hedges and walls
Leave livestock, crops and machinery alone
Take your litter home
Help to keep all water clean
Protect wildlife, plants and trees
Take Special care on country roads
Make no unnecessary noise.

Way In: From Leicester and back

VIA ANSTEY LANE LEICESTER
-GLENFRITH - ANSTEY MILL
-NEWTOWN LINFORD (4 MILES),
RETURN VIA ANSTEY. (4 MILES)

The path from Leicester that goes across fields all the way to Bradgate Park, Newtown Linford, starts from English Martyrs School on Anstey Lane, which is served by city buses.

Turn up the gravel track at the footpath sign beside the school and turn right to walk along the top hedge of the first field. Keep the hedge on your left for two fields. (The first field still has ridge and furrow visible).

There is a stile on your left at the end of the second field which leads into the remains of an old green lane. Follow this, keeping in the same direction, passing on your left Groby Road Hospital, Gilroes Cemetery and Crematorium. Cross the new road, *Glenfrith Way*, near the Severn-Trent Water Authority offices, and continue in the same direction after moving slightly right to the footpath sign and walking along the tarmac pavement which leads to a narrow grass track with the hedge on the right.

Pass Glenfrith Hospital residential area and emerge on a cross roads of paths at *Leicester Frith farm*. (A real farm, although you are still in the city boundary!).

Turn left at the farm and follow the old farm track for three fields with the hedge on your left and playing-fields beyond. Old John is now to your right. The second field has the remains of an old pond in the corner and the third (which may have crops) meets the County Boundary where the hedge swings right for a short stretch along a line of willows.

In the corner of the field cross the fence and come to a rather rough patch of ground at the start of a green lane. **(If you look carefully you will see on the ground remains of the old stone wall which was the park pale, the area enclosed to keep in the deer. The line of the pale can be seen going across the field between you and the willow tree as a raised mound.)**

Walk along the green lane and emerge on the road by No. 107. A footpath sign straight opposite leads straight on with a hedge on your right down to the footbridge over *Rothley Brook*

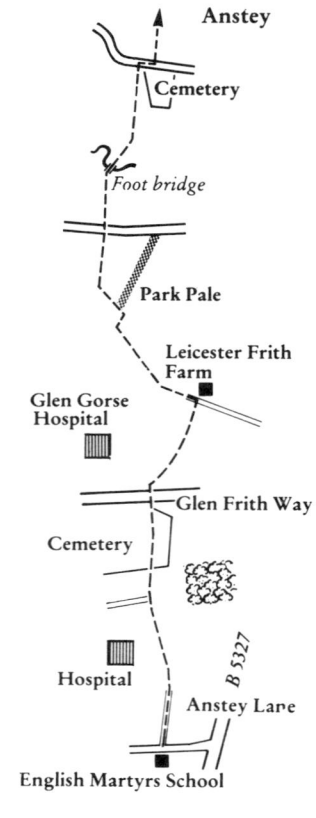

Way In: From Leicester and back

and then goes slightly right to a stile. **(Anstey Mill is on your right and an old brick bridge over the brook can be seen to your left).** Continue uphill with the hedge on your left and emerge on the road just to the left of the cemetery at Anstey.

From opposite *Anstey cemetery* walk along the farm track with the hedge on your right. At the next stile you cross the path which comes from Anstey, Manor farm and goes to Groby. Continue in your previous direction cutting across the corner of the field. Emerge in the corner of the next field (where a piece of woodland has recently been completely removed) and walk close to the hedge on your right for three large fields. Just before you reach Sheet Hedges wood the track moves to the other side of the hedge.

Walk close to *Sheet Hedges wood* on your left. In the corner of the field cross the stile which takes you through a small corner of the wood and emerge in an open field.

Move slightly right, away from the wood and walk close to the long hedge parallel to the wood, until you reach the far corner of the field. A small patch of rough ground here is all that remains of Cork Hall (marked on O.S. maps).

Cross the track (which led from Cork Hall to the farm on your right) and go across the field ahead of you to a signpost halfway along the hedge on your right. **(A farmer's sign points down the farm track to the right and then left through the gate to reach this signpost. This is sometimes the easier route to take).**

Cross the fence at the footpath sign. Walk between fences, turning right at the second F.P. sign, past farm buildings, down to the road in Newtown Linford by Stone End house. (footpath sign).

Turn left to the church and the entrance to *Bradgate Park*.

Walk through the park to *Bradgate House* ruins.

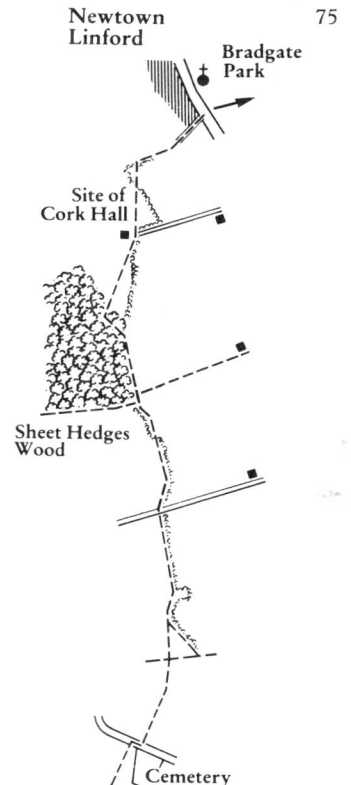

Way In: From Leicester and back

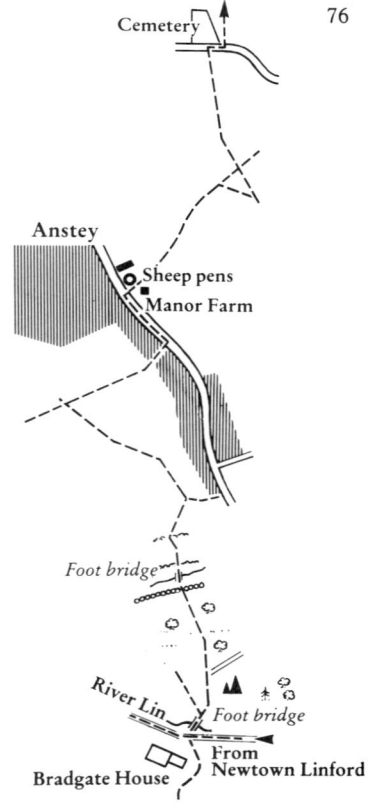

To return to Leicester from the ruins of Bradgate House, take the driveway opposite the house and cross the bridge over the River Lin. Follow the drive for 100 yards and, when it bends right to pass a little quarry outcrop, continue straight ahead (directly in line with the path which comes down from the War Memorial to the House).

Your path moves away from the river, parallel with a spinney uphill on your right. Make for the sloping green bank of the field beyond the park wall. Go through the wicket gate and up the sloping bank.

Behind you, Old John 'sits' immediately above Bradgate House chapel. Once outside the park walls, keep in the same direction, crossing a slate bridge, up to a stile in the hedge opposite. In the next, open, field pass close to a pond on your right.

Turn round to admire the view of the park. It is a view that deserves a lingering farewell!

Walk parallel with the hedge away over to your right and in the next field move to your right to the corner of the field, where a short path leads between houses to the road. You can avoid the road for a little longer by moving away from this path and from the hedge on the right to where a wooded corner juts out. Walk with this hedge on your right for two long fields. Just before you reach the houses ahead, the path swings right and goes down the middle of a long field to a gate onto the road.

There are bus stops here, but the foopath continues to be pleasant if you want to continue on foot to Leicester.

Turn left (past Link Road) and then turn right, opposite Forest Gate and cross the village green with its stone sheep-pens. Pass **Manor farm** on your left and go through the kissing gate in the corner of the green by the footpath sign.

Turn left to pass Manor farm on your left and cross the small bit of fencing which juts out in the hedge on your left. Cross a small bit of rough field and enter the narrow neck of the field ahead.

The Manor House, Groby

Way In: From Leicester and back

At the first gate, turn left and follow the hedge on your left down to the small *Anstey cemetery*. Here you join the well-used track to Anstey Lane, as described in the WAY IN walk. Crossing the footbridge and the road, go along the green lane to the junction of the county boundary and the old park pale, following the hedge on your right, to *Leicester Frith farm* and then turn right to pass the residential quarters of *Glenfrith Hospital, Gilroes cemetery* and the low brick buildings of Groby Road Hospital. The path is well defined all the way to English Martyrs School and yet retains its old world country character until the very last field, when the tower blocks of Leicester suddenly and unexpectedly appear!

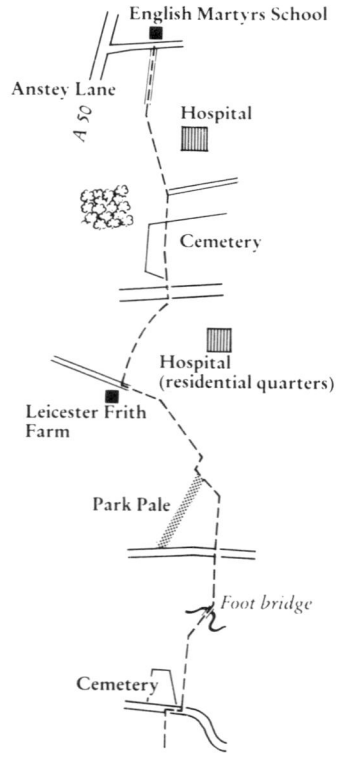

Ways In to Charnwood

Introduction
From Groby and back

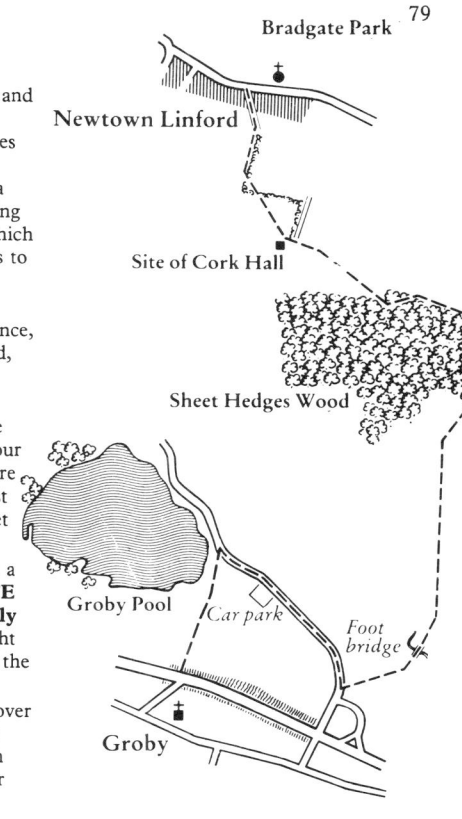

The WAY IN from Groby is a very satisfying experience because it starts from the old manor house and passes close to Groby Pool, a natural and old pool, which must have provided the manor with fish. It climbs up past Sheet Hedges wood and descends into Newtown Linford. Here one can take a tour of the park, which was the hunting park for the Greys of Groby Manor, and then return across the lovely valley between Old Wood and Lady Hay Wood. You only have to cross the A50 to reach the back of Groby, going through the beautiful Matinshaw Wood.

2 miles in: 2 miles out, with whatever you wish to add in between!

VIA GROBY POOL - SHEET HEDGES WOOD - NEWTOWN LINFORD (2 MILES) RETURN VIA MARTINSHAW WOOD (2 MILES)

From Groby Manor, opposite Ratby Road, walk uphill, pass the church and turn right along the path with the church on your right. This path goes under the A50 road, beside an old mineral railway line (which makes a pleasant alternative to the path, going between hedges to an old quarry which now serves as a car park for visitors to Groby Pool.

The footpath proper swings left, parallel to the A50 for a short distance, and then goes right, across one field, to emerge on the road near Groby Pool.

Turn right and walk back along the road, passing Groby Quarries on your left and continue as though you were going back to Groby. Turn left, just before the road forks up left to meet the A50.

The path follows the drive through a self-pick fruit farm. **(The PRIVATE KEEP OUT notice does not apply to footpath walkers.)** Keep straight on, along the drive, until you meet the stream ahead of you.

Turn left and cross the footbridge over the stream on your right. Cross the hedge in front of you and then turn left to walk with this hedge on your

Way In: From Groby and back

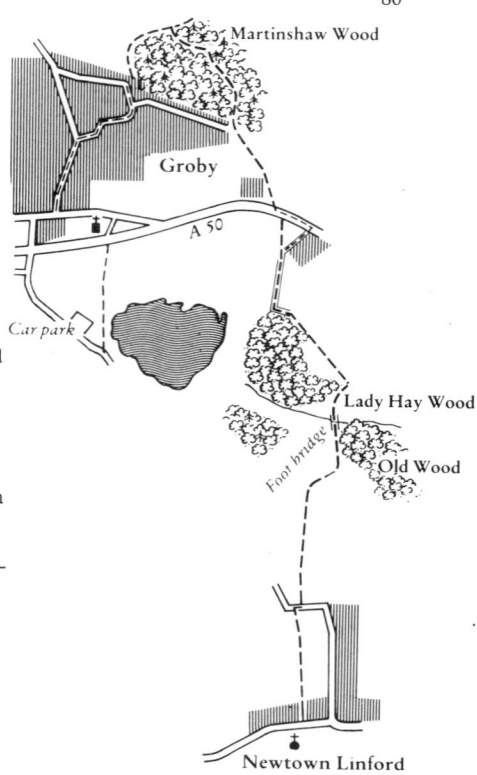

left. ***Sheet Hedges* Wood** is on the hill in front of you. Your path goes to the right top corner of it.

When the hedge on your left ends, you need to go slightly left to reach the crossing point and then slightly right to reach the corner of the wood. (The path is well marked and well-maintained.)

Turn left, to keep the wood on your left and, at the end of the field, go through a little corner of the wood. When you emerge, you need to keep in the same direction but move over to the hedge on the opposite side of the field. Walk close to this hedge, parallel to Sheet Hedges wood.

At the end of this very long field, you are level with the end of Sheet Hedges wood. An intersection of hedges marks the spot where Cork Hall stood. A rough patch of ground on your right is all that remains. A farm drive leads from it, going right to some farm buildings.

Your route crosses this drive, goes through a gap between trees, and then goes diagonally right, passing a telegraph pole in the middle of the field, to a footpath sign in the hedge on the right. **(A farmer's sign directs you down the drive and round the edge of the field to this point, and if the field is under crops this is certainly the easier route.)**

Cross the hedge by the footpath sign and walk between fencing to the next sign. Turn right and walk between barbed wire and fencing until you reach the drive to the road. (The barbed wire seems an unnecessarily unwelcoming approach to the beautiful village of Newtown Linford. Anyone snagging their expensive walking gear would be justified in complaining to the farmer and perhaps suing under the 1870 Barbed Wire Act.)

Turn left for Newtown Linford church and Bradgate park entrance.

Way In: From Groby and back

To return to Groby from Newtown Linford.

A really pretty route is to go up the path opposite the church, between two shops selling dairy ice-cream! A narrow path leads into a long, narrow field and out onto a bend in the road at the top. A gate opposite leads along a gravel track, through a gate and into a lovely old quarry area, where nature has had time to re-establish its footing. A grassy track leads through open woodland.

Where the path swings left, the track forks into two. The left fork is not a right of way, though much used by locals, as it follows the valley down to Groby Pool old boat house.

Take the right fork, keeping close to the wood on your right, then cut across the corner of the field to a bridge over the stream. Continue in the same direction across the next field to the top corner of **Lady Hay wood**. Look back to enjoy the view again!

You now enter a quarried area where nature has not yet softened the edges. Piles of granite waste and old machinery lie ahead of you. The path swings left, close to Lady Hay wood, until you emerge into a narrow gravel path, where houses back onto the wood. This path leads onto the busy A50 road.

Cross this road as best you can, and turn left along it for a short distance, to find an F.P. sign on your right at the end of the houses and beside the factory. Keep close to the hedge on your right.

A well-used track takes you uphill, towards some houses. A narrow path leads along the bottom of gardens on your left and Martinshaw woods on your right. There are lots of pretty paths through the woods. Keep to the main path, close to the left side of the wood until you reach open fields. Swing left and follow paths which take you into new housing estates, passing the school on your right.

Weave your way through the estate, back to the church on the main road in Groby.

Bradgate War Memorial from John's Lee Wood

Ways In To Charnwood
From Markfield and back

Introduction

To start the walk from Markfield you only need to cross the A50 to be in lovely open country, with fine views of Charnwood, from Copt Oak hill, surmounted by silver-gleaming radio masts, to Bradgate park, punctuated by the war memorial standing proud among the bracken. Indeed, you get this fine view even before you cross the A50 - a foretaste of joys to come!

The war memorial acts as a guide post for the first part of the route, as you walk past Cover Cloud (that beautifully named patch of woodland and Tangle Trees farm.)

As you pass John's Lee wood you may come across scouts camping as they have a permanent site here.

You have a choice of walking into Newtown Linford to do one of the walks that start there or of going straight on from the edge of John's Lee wood to join the circuit at Ulverscroft Mill. The walk down to the mill is delightful: a secluded woodland path which leads suddenly downhill to the ruined mill huddled in a dark recess by the stream.

The return from Newtown Linford covers much of the same ground. The return from Copt Oak to Markfield is described at the end of this section.

Way In: From Markfield and back

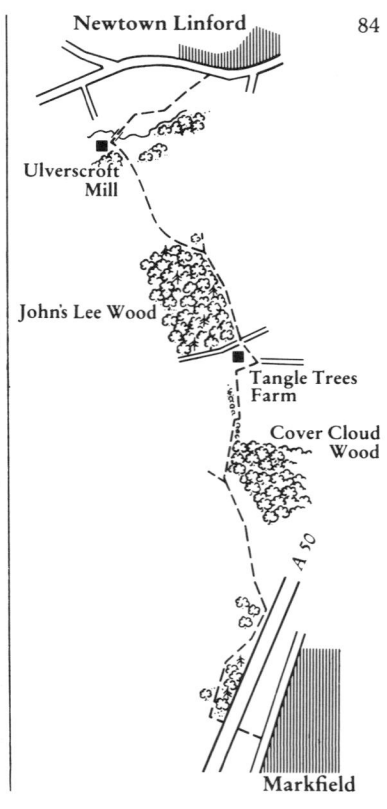

VIA COVER CLOUD - JOHN'S LEE WOOD - ULVERSCROFT MILL OR NEWTOWN LINFORD (2 MILES) RETURN FROM NEWTOWN LINFORD OR FROM WHITCROFTS LANE (SEE PAGE 85.) 2 MILES.

You can get to Markfield by bus or park your car in the village car park and walk up Main Street to the junction with the Ashby-Leicester road, by the Queen's Head pub. Turn right along the Leicester Road and pass the bus shelter. Turn left at the footpath sign opposite The Paddock.

The path begins as a tarmac strip over the first field and then goes under the A50 road. Emerge from the tunnel and swing left to a stile in the hedge ahead (passing the old overgrown stile on your right). Cross the stile and turn right. **(Do not descend to the stile below you. That is your return route.)**

Follow the hedge over some rough ground with the A50 on your right. You will need to cross a fence ahead of you (sometimes obstructed with barbed wire).

In the second field move downhill towards a belt of trees on your left. The footbridge that you need to cross is half way along the hedge which goes between the belt of trees and the A50.

Walk gradually uphill with **Cover Cloud** wood on your right. Pass close to Cover Cloud and cross the fence in the top right corner of the field. Walk with the hedge on your right towards **Tangle Trees farm**. Half way along the hedge go over the footbridge across the ditch on your right and continue in the same direction with the hedge on your left. Just before Tangle Trees farm, turn right and go to the corner of the field where there is a stile and footpath signs. Turn left and go to the right of the barn, crossing the stile and the farm track.

The path now goes beside **John's Lee wood**. At the far corner of the wood there is a path which goes straight ahead **to Newtown Linford** (waymarked as part of the Leicester Round) and one which follows the wood edge as far as a gate and then turns right, to follow the hedge on the right **to Ulverscroft Mill**.

If you wish to go to Newtown Linford and Bradgate park, leave this track at the corner of John's

Way In: From Markfield and back

Lee wood and take the J93 path to Newtown Linford by crossing the stile opposite and walk with the hedge on your left to the corner of the field. Continue in the same direction across the next field. Meet a hedge on your right and cross the fence and footbridge. Turn left and walk in the same direction to the field gate and then move diagonally right to the gate onto Markfield Lane, Newtown Linford.

If you wish to join the Ulverscroft and Copt Oak routes you can omit Newtown Linford and take the short cut via Ulverscroft Mill by passing the corner of John's Lee wood until you meet the hedge. Go through the gateway and turn right. Walk with the hedge on your right, passing a once beautiful pond (now, sadly, filled with rubbish). The path keeps close to the hedge on the right and goes gradually downhill through a wooded glade to *Ulverscroft Mill*.

To return to Markfield from Newtown Linford.

Walk along the main street of Newtown Linford for ½ mile, passing the church on your right. Take the second road on your left, signposted to Markfield. Turn right at the stile beside the gate into the first field (signposted and waymarked with the Leicestershire Round symbol).

Go uphill, diagonally, to the top right corner of the field, where the corner juts out. Keep the hedge on your right.

In the next field, 100 yards further on, there is a plank and stile to take you across into the field on your right. Follow the hedge on your left and continue in the same direction. In 100 yards the hedge ends and you need to cross the open field to the waymarked stile ahead.

In the next, small, field keep the hedge on your right and emerge in the corner of a small, usually ploughed, field with John's Lee Wood ahead of you. Go to the wood and turn left.

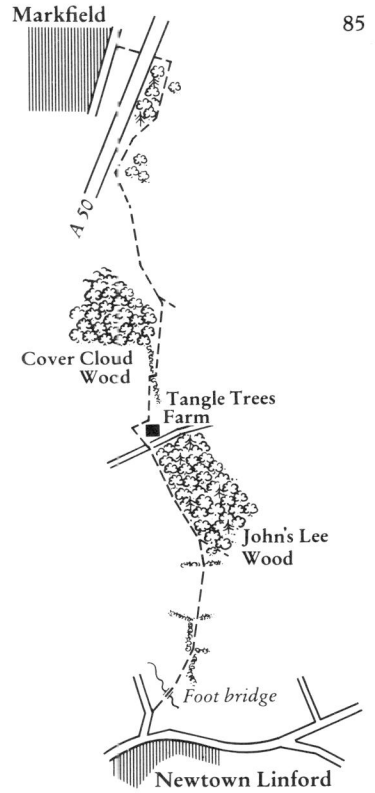

Way In: From Markfield and back

Pass the wood on your right and then continue in the same direction to cross the farm track and to pass Tangle Trees farm. At the footpath sign in the corner of the field, move over to the hedge on your right and walk along it until you come to a crossing which takes you to the other side of the hedge. Continue in the same direction, with the hedge on your left, and pass the corner of **Cover Cloud** wood. Go diagonally down to the bottom of the hill, cross the footbridge and walk towards the A50.

Turn right, to walk with the A50, on your left, until you reach the stile which leads to the path which leads under the A50 tunnel crossing.

This leads you across one field to Markfield Road, by a bus stop and close to the road junction into the village, with its shops, carparks, church and pubs. (2 miles)

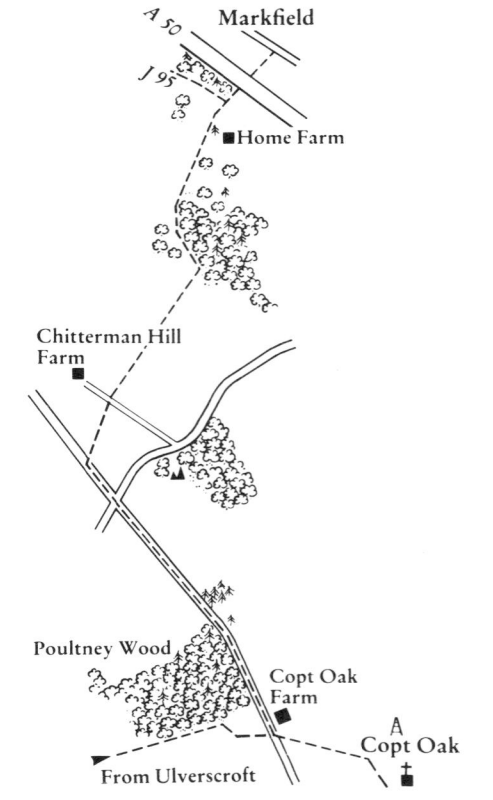

Way In: From Markfield and back

To return to Markfield from Whitcroft's Lane, Copt Oak

Turn left along Whitcroft's Lane, passing Copt Oak farm on your right. At the cross roads go straight across Priory Lane (Markfield to Ulverscroft) and walk along Lea Lane (Polly Bott's Lane) for 200 yards. Turn right at the footpath sign opposite a seat. Cross the stile in the gap in the wall and walk downhill close to the remains of an old wall on your right.

Cross Chitterman Farm lane and continue downhill for two fields, first with a wood on your right and then with a hedge on your left.

At the bottom of the second field there is a stile just to the right of the field gate. This leads you into a green track, over a slate bridge and round the edge of a spinney (Ulverscroft wood).

The track then goes between hedges to a fence. Cross the track from Home Farm and go straight ahead, passing the spinney on your right. Cross the double stile and rejoin the track uphill to cross the A50 by the tunnel provided for pedestrians.

Continue along the tarmac strip to emerge on Leicester Road, Markfield, near the Queen's Head pub. (2 miles)

Mount St. Bernards Abbey from Warren Hills

Ways In To Charnwood
From Whitwick and back

VIA RATCHETT HILL - MOUNT ST.
BERNARD'S ABBEY (2 MILES)
RETURN VIA AGAR NOOK - HOLLY
HAYS WOOD (1 MILE).

From Whitwick to Mt. St. Bernard's Abbey, is described at the beginning of walk 5 "From Whitwick, in search of an extinct volcano" (see page 67).

From Mt. St. Bernard's you can leave walk 5 and join walk 4 as on page 60 or join the Charnwood Circuit by walking along the road past the abbey to Oaks in Charnwood (1 mile) and then following the route to Lubcloud etc., as on page 51.

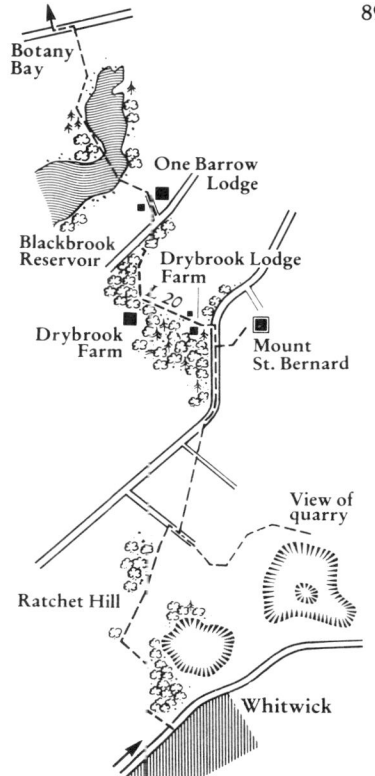

Way In: From Whitwick and back

To return to Whitwick from Agar Nook:

Cross the road opposite Agar nook housing estate and walk along Agar Nook Lane. This leads into the O22 path and continues in a straight line past playing fields on your right, across the Coalville to Shepshed road and straight on to Holly Hays Wood, on the edge of Whitwick.

You can turn right at the edge of the wood and join the main road downhill to Whitwick.

Alternatively, you can continue through the wood to emerge lower down, by walking between the stream and the houses of the former little hamlet of the City of Dan, opposite Vicarage Lane car park, Whitwick. (1 mile)

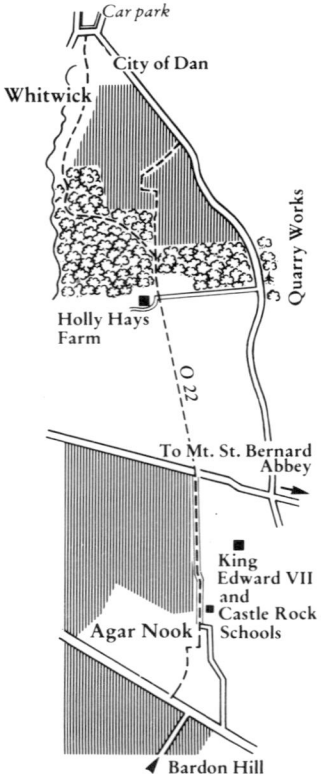

Ways In To Charnwood
From Loughborough and back

Introduction

For a very short stroll from Loughborough you can take the K57 path from Valley Road and Moat Road to Pocket Gate, walk along the edge of the Outwoods and return along the K58 path. (3 miles of gentle flatland walking on well-marked tracks and paths.)

From Pocket Gate you can add on Walk 1, by walking along a lane to Woodhouse Eaves or you can go along Dean's Lane to join Walk 2 at Beacon Hill. And, of course, from either of these points you can join the Charnwood circuit!

The route to the Outwoods provides very good views of Charnwood. It was once hedged on both sides and used as a Drift Way for stock travelling between the open fields of the village of Loughborough and the 'waste' of Charnwood, over the old deer park.

Devil's Profile, Beacon Hill from Dean's Lane

Way In: From Loughborough and back

VIA BEACON ROAD
LOUGHBOROUGH - THE OUTWOODS
- WOODHOUSE EAVES (1½ MILES).
RETURN VIA JUBILEE WOOD AND
OUTWOODS CRAG (1 MILE).

The path is a continuation of Beacon Road, Loughborough, where it meets Belvoir Drive and Valley Road. There is a car park at the end of Moat Road which leads off Valley Road, near this junction.

From the car park which is at the end of the footpath from the junction of Beacon Road and Valley Road, continue in the same direction on the very well-trodden bridle path, over the Woodbrook tributary stream, past a little recreation area on your right. To your left lies the Moat House, once a moated medieval hunting lodge in Loughborough deer park.

As you approach the Outwoods, the double hedge of the green lane becomes a single hedge on your right. It is possible to walk with this hedge on your right all the way to the handgate which leads you into the Outwoods, although this is not the official route.

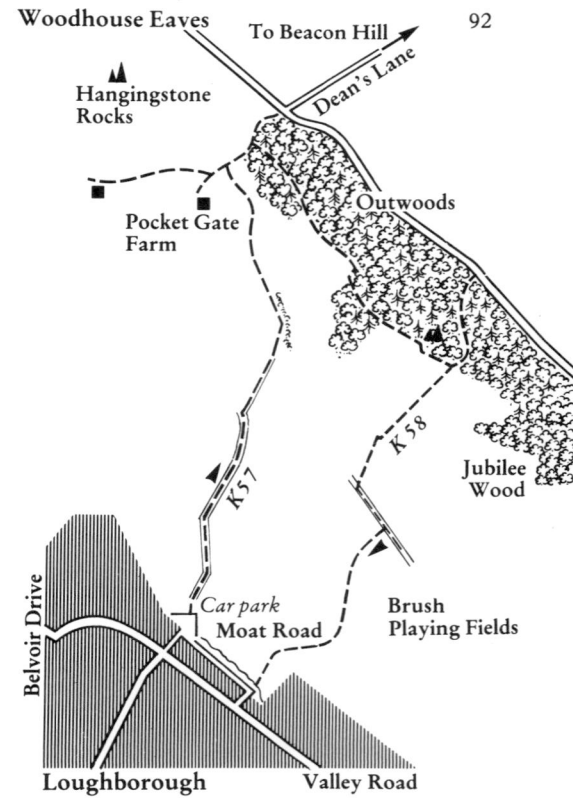

Way In: From Loughborough and back

If you wish to walk through the woods and return straight to Loughborough, turn right, after entering the woods, and walk along the edge of the wood until you reach the well-marked K58 path, where there is a seat on your left and a clear view of the path to Loughborough on your right.

If you wish to proceed to Walk 2, at Woodhouse Eaves, the official route swings left just before the Outwoods and continues past some oak trees on a track to a green lane, passing close to a War Department spinney on your right and a sheep dip on your left. Pass a house on your right and turn left along this lane.

When the lane forks to Pocket Gate farm, take the right hand fork to Woodhouse Eaves. **Ignore the misleading PRIVATE ROAD notice: it does not mean there is no footpath.** Follow the wall on your left, passing Hangingstone rocks and Golf Course on your right. Pass Hangingstone farm on your left and emerge on Brook Road, which leads into Woodhouse Eaves, opposite Ye Olde Bull's Head.

If you wish to join Walk 3 turn right to meet the main entrance to the Outwoods and cross the Woodhouse-Nanpantan Road near the junction with Dean's Lane. Walk up this lane, past Blackbird's Nest farm. At the top of the lane, turn left at the signpost to Beacon Hill, after admiring the 'devil's profile' of the hill, on your left.

1½ miles to Pocket Gate from the outskirts of Loughborough.

To return to Loughborough (1 mile)

Leave the main path which divides the Outwoods from the Jubilee Wood and go through the handgate, near a seat, which give fine open views of Loughborough. There is a fine crag near here which is used by climbers. Walk on the well-used track, following the hedge on your right until you meet Outwoods Farm Lane. Turn left for 100 yards and then turn right, keeping the hedge and Brush playing field on your left. When the hedge swings left, keep straight on to a stile opposite. The path then descends to cross the Woodbrook tributary stream and meet Moat Road.

Turn right to the car park and recreation field at the end of Moat Road or turn left to Forest Road and bus stops.

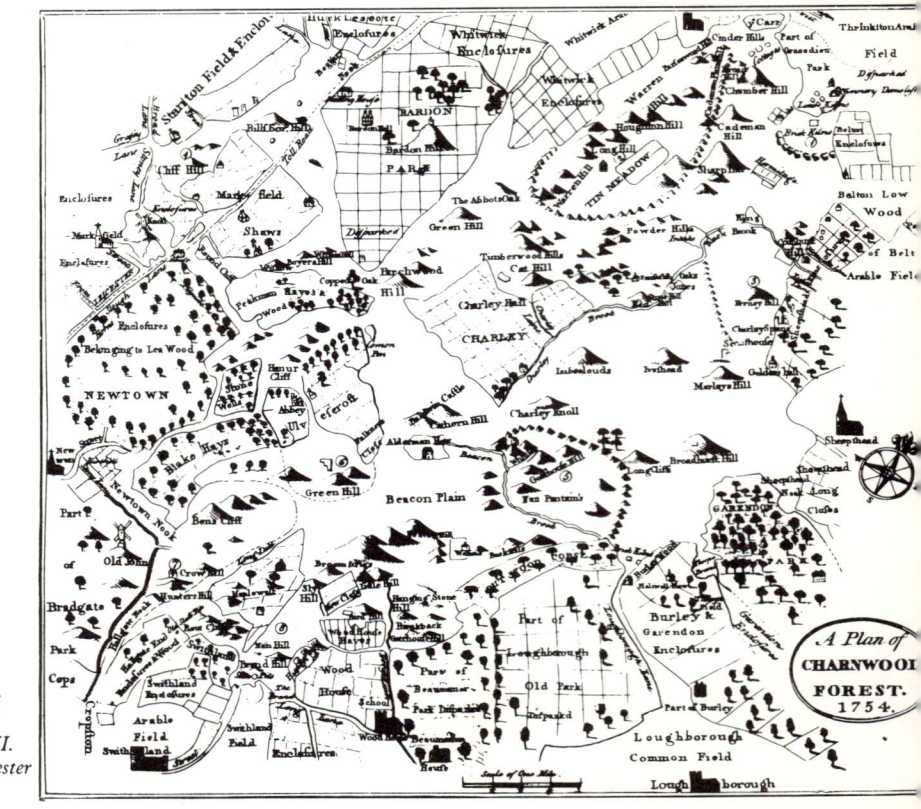

Simplified edition of Samuel Wyld's "Perambulation Round Charnwood Forrest 1754". From Nichols vol. III. The original can be seen in the Leicester Records Office (ref. DG9/Ma/66/1).

Samuel Wyld's 'Perambulation Round Charnwood Forrest 1754'

This map, produced more than 230 years ago, caught my attention because of its quality and detail and because the route it describes is similar to the route I have described in the Charnwood Circuit of this book. I was intrigued, puzzled and charmed by certain features.

Samuel Wyld, schoolmaster of Woodhouse from 1763 to 1770, completed his perambulation of Charnwood Forest in 1754. The word 'perambulation' suggests that he went on foot, and the margin of his map itemises so accurately the distance between the places he mentions that one can only assume that he carried his 'rod, pole or perch' with him to measure the ground.

By my calculation, his circuit comes to 37 miles, 2 furlongs, 32 poles. Did he really walk this as one circuit? or did he plan his route, as in this book, in overlapping circuits? Or did he arrange for horses to take him to various starting points? Did he stay the night at hostelries on the way?

Unfortunately there is no accompanying book of instructions for following his circuit and we cannot tell exactly which roads or paths he took, even though he gives us so many details.

He names in large letters the villages and towns on his route (some of which, like Markfield and Loughborough, I relegate to the 'Ways In' section of this book and others, like Stanton, Hugglescote and Belton, I omit altogether) and he names in a similarly large, but less emphatic script places of importance, neighbouring on the route.

He lists (and marks on his map) the rabbit warrens which were such a cause of complaint in January 1748/9 that troops of dragoons were called in to arrest and imprison those villagers who pulled down the rabbit warren fences because of the encroachment of the common grazing. This high drama must have been fresh in his memory when he made his perambulation.

The map itself was drawn without benefit of Ordnance Survey and although Wyld includes a North-South orientation on an impressive compass wheel, no amount of variation in magnetic north can account for the placing of Beacon Hill or Whitwick as due north of Woodhouse. It is not likely that Wyld was not aware where these places lay in relation to his schoolhouse but his map is likely to have been 'composed' to fit the space available, like the strip maps in this book. The result is a map such as a walker devoted to the area might well create. It is a 'mental picture' of the countryside.

He includes the natural features of hills and rivers and woods and the man-made features of parks, enclosures, disparked areas and rabbit warrens (which would have been fenced off to keep the rabbits in.) He marks several village streets and churches, one main toll road, from Leicester through Markfield, and his schoolhouse in old Woodhouse.

It would be interesting to have him walking our circuit with us, to give us his comments on the changes that have taken place since he drew his map but meanwhile we must be grateful to him for providing us with such a beautiful map to browse over when we have, like him, walked our circuit of the Forest.

Bibliography

Charnwood Forest: a Changing Landscape ed. J. Crocker — 1981 — Sycamore Press

A field by field survey by Loughborough Naturalists with beautiful photographs and maps and a comprehensive historical and geological survey. It includes a very full bibliography. I highly recommend it.

Commons, Forests and Footpaths Lord Eversley — 1910

Essential reading for anyone interested in the history of footpath preservation.

Charnwood Forest and its Historians, George Farnham — 1930 — Leics. Archaelog. Society

A careful study of original documentary sources. Illuminating in its detail.

Charnwood Forest C.N. Hadfield — 1952

An official survey for Leicestershire Country Council. The measured tones of the Planning Officer are perhaps unduly optimistic when he speaks of the damage being done and the council's ability to control it, but this is still a very helpful survey of the area. It has a good geological appendix and a very lively description of the volcanic forces which gave rise to Charnwood, and an account of wild life in the Forest.

The Making of the English Landscape W.G. Hoskins — 1955 — (Penguin 1973)

It is always a pleasure to read Hoskins, for his close analysis and his broad enthusiasm for the Leicestershire landscape.

The Common Lands of England and Wales L. Dudley Stamp and W.G. Hoskins — Collins 1963

Leicester and its Regions ed. Pye — Leics Univ. Press — 1972

A heavy tome, not so immediately attractive as the following books but a useful reference point.

A Family Guide to Charnwood Forest Joan Stevenson — 1982 — Sycamore Press

A Family Guide to Bradgate and Swithland Wood Joan Stevenson — 1979

Both published by Sycamore Press and available, cheaply, at information centres. Very readable summaries of most of the known facts about the area that the general reader wants to know on a brief visit. Including a bibliography of further reading.

Earlier guide books to the area are too many to mention but the ones I have referred to are:

Highways and Byways in Leicestershire J.B. Firth — 1926 — Macmillan

This has one chapter on Charnwood

Footpath Rambles with maps Leicestershire Footpath Association — 1911

Holmes of Leicester published this, price threepence!

The History Antiquitities of the County of Leicester, J. Nichols, vol. III.